Y0-BRD-096

You

Said

What?!

THE BIGGEST COMMUNICATION
MISTAKES PROFESSIONALS MAKE

KIM ZOLLER *and* KERRY PRESTON

CAREER
PRESS

Copyright © 2015 by Kim Zoller and Kerry Preston

All rights reserved under the Pan-American and International Copyright Conventions. This book may not be reproduced, in whole or in part, in any form or by any means electronic or mechanical, including photocopying, recording, or by any information storage and retrieval system now known or hereafter invented, without written permission from the publisher, The Career Press.

YOU SAID WHAT?!
TYPESET BY EILEEN MUNSON
Cover design by Howard Grossman
Printed in the U.S.A.

To order this title, please call toll-free 1-800-CAREER-1 (NJ and Canada: 201-848-0310) to order using VISA or MasterCard, or for further information on books from Career Press.

ℙ CAREER
     PRESS

The Career Press, Inc.
12 Parish Drive
Wayne, NJ 07470
www.careerpress.com

Library of Congress Cataloging-in-Publication Data

Zoller, Kim.
   You said what?! : the biggest communication mistakes professionals make / by Kim Zoller and Kerry Preston.
      pages cm
   Includes bibliographical references and index.
   ISBN 978-1-63265-010-8 (alk. paper) -- ISBN 978-1-63265-988-0 (ebook) 1. Business communication. 2. Interpersonal communication. I. Preston, Kerry. II. Title.

HF5718.Z65 2015
302.2'2--dc23
                                                          2015028905

Acknowledgments

We truly thank each other for an outstanding partnership of more than 12 years. During that time, we were lucky enough to become the best of friends. We help each other remember that we always have to continue to grow personally and we can always get better.

Many thanks to our wonderful clients and seminar participants for asking thought-provoking questions and for their active participation. This book was written with them and their colleagues in mind.

We want to acknowledge the work of Shawn Mash, Susan Klein, Paula Zeitman, and Harriet Whiting for their contributions and fascinating ideas about communication.

We thank and acknowledge our families, especially Benjamin, Samuel, Tim, Luke, Wes, and Nate.

⟩Contents

)Introduction

You can have brilliant ideas, but if you can't get them across, your ideas won't get you anywhere.

—Lee Iacocca

Wouldn't it be nice if every time the person with whom we are speaking heard us exactly the way in which we intended? Why isn't that the case more often? Things get in the way of our words. Have you ever said or heard someone say "That wasn't my intention"? Intention only means something when our communication is presented in such a way that the other person's perceptions correlate to what was intended. If they don't match, you end up with "You said *what*?"

Communication is *presence*. It is not about words or actions separately, but about how those words and actions together translate into our overall message. Presence. It is the way we present ourselves. It is how we build consistent credibility through every mode of communication.

You Said What? is a holistic view of how we communicate our message. Communication embodies many areas, and by being holistic—looking at the big picture—we ensure that we are focusing on every way we present ourselves, not on just one area. For example, communication style is a very important and "hot" topic—as it should be. If we're just focused on adapting to someone's style without taking into account what experiences they bring to the table, we may miss connecting with that person and ultimately not reach our communication goal.

It is very easy to focus on one part of communication, such as the way we speak, yet this is a very small part of what this book discusses. Focusing on one small part of communication will never get the result we're looking for. Sociologist Albert Mehrabian says that our words account for only 7 percent of the impression we make.

We are constantly communicating. We may never speak a word, but we may have said a mouthful. In almost two decades of being in this business, we have seen countless talented and intelligent individuals lose opportunities because of the way they communicated their overall messages. We have seen them fail because of the way they present themselves and the impressions they make, which correlate to their overall communication presence. On the flip side, we have also watched and followed people who "get it." They plan and they think about what they are doing and saying to make sure they are heard.

Communication is not how and what we say; it is *how we are heard*. It is not about us; it is about how the other person perceives our message and us.

Our goal for you in reading this book is that you take a step back, think about what you are really trying to accomplish, and build a plan around the way you communicate. From your words to your nonverbal communication to your brand, every single way in which you communicate can affect your outcome.

During our communication skills seminars throughout the last 19 years, we have asked more than 5,000 participants, "What are the barriers and challenges to good communication?" Here is a snapshot of their replies:

- Diversity
- Unclear direction
- Perception
- Language barriers
- Lack of knowledge
- Poor planning
- Lack of resources
- Poor listening skills
- Emotion
- Lack of approachability
- Anger
- Hidden or preconceived agendas
- Time constraints
- Preconceptions
- Ineffective verbal/written skills
- Body language
- Lack of organizational skills
- Overwhelming personality
- Intimidation
- Fear of vulnerability
- Lack of preparation
- Lack of information
- Lack of face time (shifts, geography, scheduling)
- Fear of change
- Lack of self-confidence
- Too many stakeholders
- No listening/all talk
- Fear of consequences
- Feeling that opinion matters
- Poor attitude
- Inarticulateness
- Lack of trust
- Too much jargon
- Disinterest in topic
- Inflexibility
- Different backgrounds/cultures
- Message not being communicated down the chain of command
- Different work styles
- Bad public speaking skills
- Poor nonverbal skills
- Not knowing audience
- Distractions
- People (in general)
- Unfamiliarity with material
- Confusion about end goals
- Lack of passion
- Lack of inspiration

This book has been written based on the feedback we have received. *You Said What?* is an action-oriented guide to help you reach your goal. It helps you get your message across by planning and taking the time to sharpen your communication skills.

Big Mistake 1 〉 Not Being on Your A-Game

Yesterday's home runs don't win today's games.

—Babe Ruth

What difference does one degree make? If you're hot when it's 95 degrees, you'll still be hot when it's 96 degrees. Water is extremely hot at 211 degrees, but at 212 degrees it boils. Boiling water creates steam, which is strong enough to power a train. That one degree changes the game. Imagine what it would take for you to change your game.

Thought and planning are the keys to making a difference in your communication style and approach. You have an opportunity to either make a difference or be the

"The door to success is sticking."

same as everyone else. Is it worth it to think things through a little more? One degree more? Or is the status quo easier? Being on your A-game is a mind-set. It's an overall positive attitude toward the differences you want to make in your own life and in others' lives. Think about it: If you took a step back to be solution-driven every time there was a conflict, wouldn't you be a difference-maker? Wouldn't it make life easier for you and for others around you?

You may recognize the following scenario. The plane is delayed and someone—maybe you—is not going to make his or her connection. Not only is the flight delayed, but it is also overbooked and a passenger has lost his seat. He is yelling and screaming at the airline representative. The representative looks back and says with a short and rude tone, "There is nothing I can do. Please have a seat." The passenger is furious, and the fight is just beginning.

If either the passenger or the airline representative had been on their A-game, the situation would have had a completely different sound and feel. The outcome may not change, but if the conversation was composed, empatheic, and professional, there is an 80 percent chance that either the representative would want to help or the passenger would calm down.

On the Side

"Recently I was thrilled to get on an earlier flight, which meant I was going to get home earlier after a long week away. The plane was oversold and I was put in the middle seat in the last row of the plane. I was standing in line and the woman in front of me was arguing with the gate agent about her seat. She was arguing that she was a valued customer and how dare the agent not give her a better seat. The agent was very polite and repeated, 'I'm very sorry but we have no open seats.' The lady stood there for five more minutes trying to get her to come up with another seat and the agent kept repeating the same sentence. The customer finally walked away. As I walked up I gave the agent a smile and we looked at each other with that silent acknowledgment of 'I get it; what a hassle she was!' I then talked to the agent and said with a an apologetic smile, 'I'm so glad to be on this flight and it sounds as though you have no open seats, but is there any way I can get into a better seat?' The agent looked at me, smiled, and said, 'It's all in the approach,' and gave me a great bulk head seat. You really do catch more flies with honey than vinegar. Another lesson in how you communicate to reach your goal."

—Kim Zoller, Image Dynamics

Having a positive attitude doesn't mean walking around with a big smile on your face all day, every day. It means taking a breath when something goes wrong. It means looking at worst-case scenarios and thinking about the solution rather than focusing on the problem and who caused that problem. It means being open and present, not closed to what is going on around you. It also means knowing that you can't control everything. Ultimately, it means controlling your reactions.

The bottom line is that people do not want to be around negative people. They do not want to work with people they cannot communicate with in a positive way. Things go askew at the worst of times, for instance, when we are rushed or have a deliverable that was due yesterday. We have a choice during those times to be kind to others and to not react negatively. During any meeting or seminar in which we discuss reacting versus staying calm and being kind to the people around us, the common thread is that those who are moody and reactive are perceived as less professional. No one wants to work with people who react when things go wrong.

According to a study conducted by the Carnegie Institute of Technology, 15 percent of the reason you get a job, keep a job, and move ahead in that job is determined by your technical skills and knowledge—regardless of your profession—and 85 percent is determined by your people skills and people knowledge, including your enthusiasm, smile, tone of voice, personal responsibility, and moral and ethical excellence. The outcome of our communication is driven by our ability to get along.

There are best practices throughout this book; we challenge you to use them on a consistent basis. At the end of the book, there is an action plan for continued success with a metrics checklist for you to implement. If you do implement the tools, the outcome of your interactions will change. We have tested these practices ourselves, we have observed the communications of others, and we have interviewed thousands of people about what they believe are the keys to effective communication. When we handle things while playing our A-game, we always have a positive outcome.

There is no one who describes being on your A-game better than legendary football coach Vince Lombardi, who was known for his thoughts about winning and losing. Lombardi stressed that winning was a habit and people had to play with everything they had—not only their bodies, but their heads, too. He equated the game of football to business, and in order to win in business, people need to play with their hearts, their heads, and every fiber in their bodies. That A-game was about giving it all you've got. It was about not just sticking your toe in the water, but about immersing yourself.

It makes a difference when there is a coach motivating us and getting us to think about playing to win. On a daily basis, we have to be our own coaches who motivate and drive us. Take the time to think about the outcome you are trying to achieve and always be on your A-game by following best practices. Observe others and take note of addional A-game behaviors and actions.

Best Practices

❯❯ Eliminate your own negative self-talk. Only say kind words to yourself. "I tired hard," "I learned from that," "I give my all in situations." (We found that negative self-talk happens at every level and every age. The most successful people with the most successful communication are mindful of this and turn it around as soon as they realize it is happening.)

❯❯ Be aware of how your mind can create a negative situation that does not really exist. Keep those thoughts in check. (See Big Mistake 10: Making Assumptions.)

❯❯ Be aware of mental distortions that hurt your A-game. (See Big Mistake 10: Making Assumptions.)

❯❯ Monitor your tone. Avoid sounding sarcastic, dictatorial, condescending, or arrogant. If you are not sure how you are coming across, ask someone you trust for feedback. Or better yet, become aware of how others are reacting to you.

❯❯ Try to understand where the other person is coming from. Empathy is asking yourself, "How would I feel if I were in this situation?"

❯❯ Listen to others. Can you remember what someone said five minutes after the conversation? Stop thinking and start listening. Avoid thinking about other things while others are talking.

❯❯ Be prepared. Spend time planning communication so that you utilize the "intellectual" part of your brain, which allows you to evaluate. Avoid using the "reptilian" part of your brain, which allows you to react without thinking.

❯❯ Set goals for your interactions with others. Before going into any interaction, plan out how you will behave to meet your own A-game goal.

▶ Focus on things that make a difference. Pay attention to where you are spending your internal energy. If you are emotional about something, ask yourself if it is worth all the focus or if the energy could be put into something constructive.

▶ Try to offer help to others. Remember that the more you help other people, the more you will get back in return. It is not all about "me."

▶ Stay calm. Create techniques that help do this. Breathe in and exhale out in twice the time you spent breathing in. Relax your shoulders and facial expressions.

▶ Plan out hypothetical worst-case scenarios. This includes any potential risks that may occur or key insights from past experiences.

Ask Yourself These Crucial Questions

▶ Have I seen an outcome turn from negative to positive based on the way I handled the situation?

▶ Am I affected by someone else's negative attitude? Have I communicated differently because of that negative attitude? How has that affected my A-game?

▶ Have I ever lost a job or a promotion when I thought my skills were a perfect fit? What am I not seeing?

Big Mistake 2 〉 Not Beginning With the End in Mind

All that we are is the result of what we have thought.

—Buddha

Think before you speak. This is such a basic concept, yet it is so hard to put into practice. Everything we say has a consequence—positive or negative. If we don't know our big-picture goal, our communication can affect the outcome in a negative way. If we know our goal and we think through the "why," "what," and "how," we have a better chance of affecting our relationships in a positive way. There are spontaneous conversations, and there are conversations for which we have time to plan and think through while keeping the end goal in mind.

On the Side

"A colleague of mine recently said he was upset that I didn't include him in a meeting he thought he should have been invited to. This was a spontaneous conversation where someone was upset with me, and I didn't have an opportunity to plan my response. I could have reacted and responded in many different ways. Engaging in a

negative way could have created other problems. This situation made me realize I need to be mindful of the words I use to achieve my goals."
—Social media manager for an events company

If someone does something that you don't like or agree with, do you tell them? Well, what is your goal? Do you know what actually happened, or are you making assumptions about what happened? If you say something, what will the outcome look like? Is there a potential to create problems and break down a long-term relationship because of a judgment or feeling you have? Be aware that some bridges can never be rebuilt.

Different parts of our brain dictate how we behave. Without getting into the specifics of the brain and the accompanying studies, let's discuss how the brain has an effect on keeping the communication goal in mind at all times. Our brain has three areas: the two that we will discuss here (and were mentioned in the previous chapter), are the intellectual and reptilian/animal parts of the brain. When we do not have a "goal in mind," we open a window to react at will.

> ### *Definition of Emotional Intelligence*
> "Emotional intelligence is the ability to perceive emotions, to access and generate emotions so as to assist thought, to understand emotions and emotional knowledge, and to reflectively regulate emotions so as to promote emotional and intellectual growth."
> —John Mayer and Peter Salovey, developers of the theory of emotional intelligence

When we plan ahead, we are in control of those basic brain reactions. In business, those reactions rarely have a positive outcome. How does one put the intellectual part of the brain into play and lower the chances of the animal part just reacting? Plan ahead. Think about the conversation you are about to have. Write down all of the negative things that can come out of it and how the other person may react. Think through the reactions and how you would respond accordingly to meet your goal. This is how you grow your emotional intelligence in the workplace.

On the Side

"Planning conversations allows you to cultivate the skills you need to identify and align your goals with those of the person you are meeting with, and to best articulate your plan in a way that lends itself to the preferred communication style of your audience. By nature, I am an incredibly emotional and sensitive person. I take things personally, and the majority of the time, 'words hurt' the most. I found myself unable to communicate the way I was thinking because it was clouded by the way I was 'feeling.' I was repeatedly unable to get my point across, no matter how valid or well supported, because I was coming across as upset or excited, and the people I was trying to get buy-in from had already disregarded my point within the first five minutes of our conversation.

"Learning how to effectively plan conversations has truly revolutionized the way I interact in the corporate world. It has allowed me the ability to communicate most effectively depending on the goals of every single conversation that I have. I've become far more productive, my relationships with my teammates have improved, and I'm developing a more professional and respected reputation with my peers and leadership alike. Taking a few extra minutes to plan your conversations really goes a long way!"

—Alexandra Wilinksi, Capgemini

Best Practices

➧ Realize that the past can affect someone's perception about a situation.

- When possible, plan your conversation to make sure your communication matches your goal.

- Plan out the negative reactions that could occur and how you are going to handle not getting triggered from the other person's reaction.

- Think about your timing and its effects; the context of a situation can affect everything.

- Everyone has their own agenda; look at both sides.

- Seek clarity before making assumptions.

- Think before you speak. Even when you are put on the defensive, remember your goal.

- Think about what you will achieve by saying something.

Ask Yourself These Crucial Questions

- Have I wished that I could take back something I said to a colleague?

- If I could change the outcome, what would I do differently the next time? What did I learn?

- How can I better manage my reactions and emotions to reach my communication and relationship goals?

Big Mistake 3 〉 Not Knowing Your Personal Brand

Regardless of age, regardless of position, regardless of the business we happen to be in, all of us need to understand the importance of branding. We are CEOs of our own companies: Me, Inc. To be in business today, our most important job is to be head marketer for the brand called You.

—Tom Peters

How do personal branding and communication go together? Everything you say—verbally and nonverbally—is your brand. If you don't think you have a brand, you're wrong. You do. Others expect you to communicate a certain way based on their past experiences with you. How you send e-mails, when you text, how you deal with problems, how you give compliments, and how you take criticism are just a few examples of how you have already branded yourself.

In the previous chapter, we explored your goal. Branding yourself is 100 percent tied into that goal and is a critical component of being heard. Before we go further, think about the goal you have in mind. Which of your behaviors support that goal?

Are you consistent? You build your brand through consistently communicating what people can expect from you. Build and market your brand rather than letting others decide it for you.

We must invest in our brands. Everything from how we look, what we learn, how we grow, and our personal and professional development are components of our investment. These are all areas for you to invest in, to protect your brand.

Go into the lobby of any hotel or place of business and observe the surroundings. You can immediately describe that entity's brand. Your dress is your brand's decor. People notice you and can describe you, yet you haven't said a word.

Because we work in a very image-driven business world, we notice how much attention successful individuals apply to their brand. It's attention to detail and consistency, and it requires forethought and taking that extra step to make sure that all of our communications send the same message.

On the Side

"I was conducting a seminar for a large manufacturing company, and one of the executives told me a story of how he had once said to his boss that he liked what he was doing and didn't want to be a manager. His boss branded him, and while he worked for her, he was never promoted. He now realizes how he built that brand and wasn't able to readjust until he changed departments."

— Kim Zoller, Image Dynamics

Changing a negative opinion of you can be very difficult. Once you have made a negative impression, you have to make one positive impression after another, which can be difficult if you do not have the chance to do that. In fact, a 2009 study by the Department of Psychology at Harvard University was published in an article in *Nature Neuroscience* that stated it will take eight subsequent positive encounters to change a person's negative impression of you if their initial impression of you was negative. The following ideas might help avoid the negative first impression.

▶ Your brand has to be adaptable to your environment and situation but authentic to yourself. Take into account personalities, culture, and your surroundings, and adapt to them without losing yourself.

▶ Opt for quality rather than quantity with wardrobe selection. A book is judged by the cover before the words are read. Take the time to make sure that you are representing how you want people to see you.

▶ Live your brand every day; it makes a difference. This is the same for your attire, demeanor, and behavior. Consistency builds your brand.

▶ Don't forget that even details like e-mails support or detract from your brand, so reread everything you write. This is a permanent record of how you are seen.

▶ Select words that build your brand and stay away from slang. Avoid words like "huh," "gonna," "yup," and "yea."

▶ Stay away from negative chitchat; you can destroy your brand through negative talk and gossip. The minute your name gets attached to something that was said about someone else, you have the chance of being branded as the "office gossip." This can ruin a reputation that is difficult to build back. It also jeopardizes relationships and burns bridges that can never be rebuilt.

▶ Put your best foot forward. Each day is a new day. Make it strong by thinking about your goals and planning ahead.

On the Side

"My colleague Sam was the smartest guy in the room. The problem was that I didn't want to take him to client meetings because I never knew if he was going to be dressed professionally or look as though he had just woken up. I didn't have the nerve to say anything to him, I just didn't include him."

—Frank S., consultant in wireless industry

A systematic approach to building a positive brand is important to drive your future success. Let's take a look at a cost-benefit analysis of a strong brand versus an inconsistent brand.

Cost of negative brand	Benefit of positive brand
• Inability to be promoted.	• Promotability.
• Unfavorable impression leading to loss of business.	• Positive impressions leading to growth of business, trust, and stronger relationships.
• Lack of respect.	
• People do not listen to your ideas.	• Respect from colleagues.
• Attitude of indifference toward you.	• Being heard when sharing ideas and thoughts.
• Inability to get referred for a new job.	• Being referred internally and externally for projects/jobs.
• Inability to lead a team effectively.	• Having more influence with others and over situations.
• Lack of trust and confidence in your abilities.	

What habit or behavior do you want to change to improve your brand? Is the cost worth it to you to change your behavior? Do you feel that staying with what you currently do will help you grow, improve, and succeed?

Take an element of your brand, a specific behavior, and weigh the cost-benefit for that behavior and how it is helping or hurting your career.

On the Side

"Three months after going through our program a client of ours called to share the impact of her personal rebranding effort. She said that she had changed her attire to still edgy but more professional, had changed how she reacted and no longer raised her voice, and had also started reading every e-mail to make sure there were no typos and her writing was professional. The impact was manifested through more of her colleagues coming to her for advice and guidance."

—Susan B., high potential associate at a toy and gaming corporation

Best Practices

▶ Your behavior needs to be consistent at least 90 percent of the time. People will give you a break once in a while (about 10 percent of the time) if you have built a positive brand.

▶ Think about people who are professional 50 to 60 percent of the time. What happens to the other 40 to 50 percent of that time? Not being consistent leads to an ambiguous brand, which translates into a lack of trust.

▶ A negative brand takes consistent behavior over time to adjust others' thoughts.

Ask Yourself These Crucial Questions

▶ Do all of my communications support my personal brand? Am I living my brand every day through every interaction?

▶ Do I have a mentor or someone I respect in business? What is their brand? How is their communication consistent?

▶ How can I tie in my daily interactions and tasks with my personal brand initiative?

Big Mistake 4 〉 Not Managing Perceptions

There are things known and there are things unknown,
and in between are the doors of perception.

—Aldous Huxley

Perceptions affect the outcome of our communication. The way we walk, the way we hold ourselves, the way we dress, how we carry our briefcase, the look of the briefcase, our smile (or lack of one)—the list could go on. The impression we make on other people often determines how well they communicate with us. Bad first impressions generally lead to bad relationships. Good first impressions give us the opportunity to build rapport and establish good two-way communication.

What makes perception reality is that we are dealing not only with our communication efforts but also with the experiences of the receiver of the communication.

In 1955, the Johari Window, a cognitive psychological tool, was created by sociologists Harry Ingham and Joseph Luft. The Johari Window is used to help people better understand their interpersonal communications and relationships. It gives us an understanding of how people may hear things differently from how we intended, and it also helps us look at our own self-awareness and how that self-awareness affects our overall communication.

With this understanding, if we have good and open communication with people, we can solicit feedback to help us grasp how we are heard and perceived.

Johari Window

	Things You Know About You	Things You Don't Know About You
Things Others Know	Public Knowledge Open/Free Area	Blind Spot Blind Area
Things Others Don't Know	Secret Unknown Area	Unknown Potential Unknown Area

"The Johari window, a graphic model of interpersonal awareness."
Reprinted from Joseph Luft and Henry Ingham.

To understand the Johari Window, it is important to recognize that:

▶ Public Knowledge/Open/Free Area represents what we know about ourselves and what others know about us.

▶ Blind Spot/Blind Area represents what others notice about us that we do not realize.

▶ Secret/Unknown Area represents things that we have not and do not want to share with others.

▶ Unknown Potential/Unknown Area represents what we do not know about ourselves and what others do not know, either. This area is generally explored in therapy.

On the Side

The following story was told to us by one of our clients after she learned about the Johari Window:

"One day a woman I've known for a long time called me. She is the mother of a child at the school my kids attend. She has never said a word to me. She hardly even looks at me when I pass her in the parking lot or in the school hallway. We have been at many of the same functions and parties, and she has never smiled or spoken to me—just completely ignored me. In fact, every time someone introduces us, she looks at me as though she has not met me at least ten times before.

"I have always been totally put off by her and have always thought she was rude. So when my phone rang and it was her, I was extremely surprised that she even knew my name. She asked if she could come in to discuss something with me and I said yes. I was curious to hear what she had to say. Well, she was looking for a job. The most interesting thing about the conversation was that she went on and on about how people always tell her that she should be in a position where she is around people, how great she is around people, and that she has been told that she has the most endearing personality. I wanted to say to her, 'Are you sure they were talking about you?'"

—Leadership development director

This woman was definitely in the Blind Spot of the Johari Window.

Self-perception can be a strange thing if there's no awareness, self-reflection, or feedback from people you trust. It is hard to have a good channel of communication when people perceive you differently from how you perceive yourself. In Chapter 12 we will adress giving and receiving feedback.

Best Practices

Attire

❥ Dress appropriately every day for every situation.

❥ Think before you wear something that may convey the wrong message.

❥ Do not risk losing respect just to be comfortable.

❥ Think about who you might meet or see and whether your attire represents your brand.

Body Language

Your body language speaks volumes about your feelings or others' perceptions of your feelings. Be aware of what you are communicating without even opening your mouth.

❥ Keep your shoulders back and your head up.

❥ Have a firm and appropriate handshake.

❥ Hold eye contact when shaking someone's hand.

❥ Make eye contact and do not look around when engaged in conversation.

❥ Smile when appropriate.

❥ Do not fidget with your hair, pen, change in your pocket, or anything else that will distract from what you are saying.

Conversation

❥ Stay positive; do not talk about negative things.

❥ Maintain a good attitude.

❥ Be prepared.

❥ Stay focused—be present.

❥ Be concise; do not chatter.

❥ Be interested, not interesting.

Meetings

▶ Verbal and nonverbal communication speak loudly in meetings.

▶ Speak up and be present.

▶ Speak with confidence when you have something to add, not just to talk.

▶ Introduce yourself. You are your brand.

Body Language That Gets in Your Way

▶ When you walk around with a serious look all the time, people assume you have too much on your plate and that you are not approachable. The solution: smile.

▶ When you are disorganized and harried all the time, people assume you cannot handle your work. The solution: clean your desk, slow down, look up, and breathe.

▶ Be aware of:

   ▶ Sounds of verbal frustration (for example, "tsk").

   ▶ Heavy sighs.

   ▶ Crossed arms.

   ▶ Eye rolling and eye fluttering.

   ▶ Looking down.

   ▶ Head shaking.

Ask Yourself These Crucial Questions

▶ What are the five words other people use to describe me?

▶ Am I perceived the way I want to be perceived? If there is a gap, what actions can I take to close that gap?

▶ How do I become more self-aware? What type of feedback do I need to seek out from someone I trust?

Big Mistake 5 \ Not Connecting and Building Relationships

The most important single ingredient in the formula of success is knowing how to get along with people.

—Theodore Roosevelt

This chapter addresses two topics: the personal and emotional connections we make with others and how we network to build connections. These topics are tied together very closely.

"I know that I wronged you on the way up, but I'm much nicer now that I'm here."

Companies spend billions of dollars on marketing and public relations in order to build trust and likeability of their brand or product. Similarly, millions of people go to networking groups to establish connections that build trust and likeability so that they can do business or be referred. We create value by building connections, and we build value in ourselves by connecting with other people on a personal level.

Are you connecting with those around you? Communication is about the connections we make with others and how those connections represent you to others. Connecting is very important; just look at the success of LinkedIn or any of the other social media websites that help make connecting easier.

On the Side

"Recently I walked into a jewelry store and saw something I loved. I didn't know the store or the owner, who was helping other customers. The store looked busy and people seemed to be buying, so I thought it was probably a reputable place, but I wanted to make sure. I pulled out my phone and used Google to check reviews about the store. Within minutes I found a bad review from the Better Business Bureau. I walked right out. Keep in mind that that review could have been the result of just one person's complaint. It's unfortunate, but it speaks to how closely we are all connected."

—Real estate agent

We build trust by doing great work. We also build trust by being recommended by our network. It is always better for someone to tell someone else how great we are than to tell that person ourselves. They believe it far more when it comes from another source. As you work toward your goals, keep in mind how everyone is interconnected. When you build bridges, it is easier to get to someone through someone who already knows and trusts you.

Building Bridges

Are you building bridges? If something negative has happened with someone, remember that they too have a network and that we are all only separated from one another by a few degrees.

⮞ Apologize if you have done something that another person has perceived negatively.

➧ Do what you can to remedy the situation.

➧ Do not go over anyone's head to get to another person unless you have thought through the situation and you know the outcome will be what you want.

➧ Do not go over someone's head just to get immediate results.

➧ If you do go over someone's head, be aware that you may burn one bridge to build another.

➧ Be inclusive. Do not purposefully leave colleagues out of e-mails, meetings, and social events related to work. Being inclusive also requires the use of forward thinking to include others who may be impacted.

➧ When working on a project, make sure you are including everyone in e-mails and other group conversations.

Networking

Are you using your channels to network and communicate your message?

➧ Keep in touch with people you meet.

➧ Follow up with a phone call or a note when you have made a good connection.

➧ Don't only follow up with someone when you need something.

➧ Introduce people to other people who can help them achieve their goals.

➧ Don't be afraid to ask someone to refer you to someone else if you have a good relationship.

➧ Prove yourself through top-notch work before you ask someone to do anything for you.

➧ Be there when people need you.

Elevator Speech

Can you explain who you are in 99 seconds or less? It's hard to come up with an elevator speech if you don't know your brand. There are two types of elevator speeches: one for telling someone what you do and another for when someone asks you how you are and what you've been doing lately. You have to prepare and practice both and realize that your elevator speeches can determine the longevity of the conversation.

The key elements of your elevator speech are:

▶ Your full name.

▶ Your position.

▶ Something interesting you do that is quickly explained, easy to understand, and applicable to that person.

▶ Your aspirations.

Answering "What do you do?"

▶ Be brief and be clear.

▶ Try to relate what you do to something the person knows about. For example, ask a question to see if he or she is familiar with the type of work you do, such as:

   ▶ "Have you ever been to a training workshop on building your communication skills? That's what I do."

   ▶ "Does your company have a corporate university? I have a corporate training company where we do everything from writing a business process, training that process, writing and developing corporate universities, and training personal and professional development skills like communication."

   ▶ "Were you recruited before joining your company? I am the Human Resources director for Big Star, and I handle all the employee benefits and recruiting."

Putting It Together

Steve: Kerry, what do you do?

Kerry: I am a partner in a company called Image
         Dynamics. Have you ever been to a leadership
         training workshop or read any leadership books?

Steve: Yes, all the time. My company just sent me to a great
         course.

Kerry: That's what I do. I work with companies to develop
         their people and processes, as well as write business
         books on personal and profession development.

Keep in mind that you need to tailor your elevator speech to your audience. For example, talking to an external customer is different from talking to a key decision-maker in your company. Again, the key is that your applicable question must be something that the person will be able to relate to or do. If it isn't, reframe your question. This allows the receiver to truly understand what you do and opens the doors of interest and communication.

Answering "How are you? What have you been doing lately?"

▶ Always be positive; no one wants to hear bad news.

▶ Thank the person for asking.

▶ Don't forget to reciprocate and ask the person how they are doing.

▶ Repeat the question to buy some time while you formulate an answer. "What have I been up to? That's a good question..."

▶ Be ready to discuss some exciting things going on at work, but try not to sound like you are bragging. For example:

  ▶ "I am doing well, thanks. Business has been really fun lately; I have been working on two big projects."

  ▶ "I am well, thanks. Luckily, we are very busy and I have been meeting with some new clients and finding out their needs. I love that part of my job."

Establishing Your BLT

Establishing believability, likeability, and trust (BLT) is crucial to communicating your overall message. How do we do that?

▶ Be positive in all situations and stay on your A-game.

▶ Say only positive things about other people. If you say negative things about someone else, the listener will automatically assume that you will say negative things about them, too.

▶ Do not speak badly about your competitors.

▶ Do what you say you are going to do every time.

▶ Follow up in a timely manner.

▶ Apologize when you do not follow through or follow up when you said you would.

▶ Be interested in others, not interesting.

Putting It All Together: Tapping Into Your Network

You have made the effort to network and get out there. You are ready with your elevator speech and answering the easy questions. Now what? You have to get to the next layer, which is where the relationship will truly be built.

The following techniques will help you before, during, and after having a conversation with someone.

Before

▶ Know your goal of engaging. We personally approach each situation with a positive and open outlook. True business success is about give and take, and walking into every interaction with an open mind and willingness to share. "Pay it forward" is a core value that we embody in all interactions. For instance, when I go to a meeting or event, I always have two main questions:

1. "What can I learn from the people I talk to/meet?"

2. "How can I learn more about each person so that I build a relationship that will help me grow my business and help them with theirs?"

During

▶ Be engaged and don't think about what is going on around you.

▶ Even if you are not interested in the person at the onset, you never know how truly interesting someone is until you delve a little deeper. Stay nonjudgmental.

▶ Think of your conversation and questioning techniques as a way to delve.

▶ Think of your questions like branches on a tree. Each question is a main branch. If the other person engages and answers the question with more than a one-word answer, build another branch question off the main branch.

▶ If you go from one main branch to the other, the conversation will not flow and will seem disjointed.

▶ If a person answers the question with a short answer and you get the feeling that they do not want to engage in that topic, move on to another main branch question.

▶ Allow the conversation to go back and forth between you and the other person. If you find that you are talking too much, turn it around.

After

▶ Follow up with the people you talked to at the event or meeting.

▶ If you said you would do something, do it immediately. As our mentor Walter Hailey would say, "Always do what you ought to do, when you ought to do it. No debate!"

▶ Write a note expressing your appreciation for the conversation.

▶ Put the person in your database and remind yourself to check in with him or her on a regular basis. This will be determined by the situation.

❧ If the person is someone you do not see on a regular basis or you just met, be sure to schedule a next action.

Best Practices

❧ If you are meeting someone for the first time, stand up, shake their hand, make eye contact, smile, and introduce yourself with your full name, company, and position.

❧ Notice eye color; this helps you maintain eye contact.

❧ Stay positive.

❧ If they don't introduce themselves back, simply ask with a smile on your face, "What's your name? Where do you work?"

❧ Be prepared with questions to ask others.

❧ In any corporate environment, know who the key players and executives are.

On the Side

As you can see, networking is crucial to one's success. Whether it is inside or outside a company, building strong relationships affects one's success. Manpower Group, a Milwaukee-based staffing company, conducted a survey analyzing 59,133 of their clients over the last three years. Of those clients, 41 percent said they landed a job through networking.

Ask Yourself These Crucial Questions

❧ Is there a bridge that I have burned that I need to rebuild? If yes, what is my timeline and action plan to rebuild it? What am I going to do from this point forward to ensure I do not burn a bridge?

❧ What am I going to say the next time I am at an event where someone asks me, "What do you do?" What is my answer when someone asks me, "How are you?" or "What's new?"

❧ What techniques am I using to keep in touch and build my network? If I don't have any, what can I do to change that? Have I written notes to people who have helped me through the years? Is it time to start?

Big Mistake 6 \ Not Making Appropriate Small Talk

Talk low, talk slow, and don't talk too much.

—John Wayne

How many times have you been in a situation in which you couldn't believe what someone was saying to you? There are too many times when people make assumptions about others and offend without realizing that they're doing so. Also, building rapport in business does not mean telling everyone your personal information.

MY NEW YEAR'S RESOLUTION IS TO STOP PUTTING MY FOOT IN MY MOUTH ALL THE TIME... I'LL BET YOURS IS LOSING WEIGHT, HUH?

Do your research. Know who you're talking to and be careful if you do not. Be prepared with topics to discuss so that you can engage in a meaningful conversation. Ask "how," "what," and "why" questions to learn more about the other person and keep the conversation going. Clearly, rapport is not about "putting someone on the stand." It is more like a tennis match, going back and forth. It is about being genuine and authentic, and realizing that finding common ground builds long-term relationships. Some good ice-breaker questions and topics are:

- ▶ "How did you get involved...?"
- ▶ "Tell me more about..."
- ▶ "What are some of the challenges you face?"
- ▶ "What do you enjoy most about...?"
- ▶ "When did you start...?"
- ▶ "How did you prepare for...?"
- ▶ "What's next for you?"

Some examples of topics to discuss are:

- ▶ Career background.
- ▶ Achievements and goals.
- ▶ Hobbies and leisure activities.
- ▶ Community involvement.
- ▶ Entertainment (favorite movies and books).
- ▶ Current events (as long as they are not controversial).
- ▶ Family (as long as the other person brings it up first; do not get too personal).

Remember that just because you are a good talker does not mean that you are a good *small* talker. It takes practice and a willingness to learn about and enjoy other people. Let go of the anxiety over what you have to say and become interested in others. It is amazing how important a person feels when someone is interested in them.

Best Practices

Certain topics will definitely come up at some point while you are holding conversations with others. Your depth of discussion on the topic should be based on your relationship with the person. At the same time, keep in mind that while you think you may have a good rapport, strong opinions on a topic can harm a business relationship. Avoid getting into discussions on the following topics:

- Politics.
- Religion.
- Sexism.
- Racist or ethnic comments.
- Sexual orientation.
- Salary.
- Gossip.
- Negativism.
- Private matters.
- Private family matters.
- Giving too much personal information.
- Giving an overabundance of detail.
- Interrogating rather than conversing.
- Interrupting the other person.
- Complaining.
- Trying to "one-up" the other person.
- Glancing around the room while someone is conversing with you.

On the Side

"I was incredibly close with one of my coworkers, Maxine. We really told each other everything, personal and professional. Last year Maxine was promoted, and everything seems to have changed. I regret telling her a lot of the things I told her. I feel that I am not being promoted because she thinks that I do not have a stable home life. I'm not sure what to do about it, but I have definitely learned to keep my personal life personal."

—Employee of an insurance company

(You can find additional tips for making small talk in *You Did What? The Biggest Blunders Professionals Make.*)

What if a colleague wants to engage with you on these topics? The following dialogue examples can give you ideas on how to disengage in the situation:

Conversation 1

Fred: Kim, what do you think about the president and his stance on what is going on right now?

Kim: It's really interesting. I'm staying away from that topic! (And then change the subject to something like, "How was your weekend?" or "How is that project going?")

Conversation 2

Rosa: Kerry, did you hear about what was going on with the head of sales and the head of marketing?

Kerry: I didn't, but office politics can get very interesting." (And then change the subject to something like, "Let's talk about the performance of brand x. It looks like it is doing really well.")

On the Side

"I was recently having a conversation with a long-term client about the election. This client and I have had 15 years of working together and I really felt as though I could share my personal opinion of the situation. Well, as soon as I shared that opinion, I realized I had made a mistake. Her body language completely closed up and the smile was gone from her face. It was evident that I had said something that triggered her personal belief and we had differing opinions. I apologized for offending her, but I do think that it has caused some negative feelings around our business dealings."

—Sales executive at an insurance brokerage

Using the phrase "that's interesting" helps ease the tension and keeps the other person from feeling uncomfortable. At the same time, it is a connector to help you change the subject.

Ask Yourself These Crucial Questions

▶ If someone were telling me the same thing I'm telling them, would I think it was appropriate?

▶ Is this person really interested in what I am saying?

▶ Am I going to regret saying this at a later date?

To finish up the thoughts in this chapter, we look to Bernardo J. Carducci, who has some good thoughts on this topic. In his book *The Pocket Guide to Making Successful Small Talk: How to Talk to Anyone, Anytime, Anywhere About Anything*, he states: "Small talk is the starting point of all relationships. Although by calling it small talk, we actually perpetuate the notion that it is trivial and unimportant. Further, it is the cornerstone of civility, as it enables contact, which discourages mistreatment of others. Many people think small talk is an innate talent. It is, in fact, an acquired skill. There is a structure and there are rules of engagement. Once individuals know the basic structure and rules for making small talk, connecting with others can become less intimidating." (Pocket Guide Publishing, 1999)

On the Side

"One of my biggest pet peeves is when vendors share their personal lives with me. I have too much to do and not enough time, and it is a waste of my time. I think there should be a book for salespeople and vendors titled *Know When to Stop Talking!* Now I just tell those specific vendors that I have exactly five minutes. I enjoy getting to know people, but some people just take it too far."

—Purchasing manager of a major airline

Meltdown of Communication Through Technology Use

E-mail is a unique communication vehicle for a lot of reasons. However, e-mail is not a substitute for direct interaction.

—Bill Gates

All of us have been the victims of miscommunication through technological outlets. Simply put, one of the largest causes of this problem comes from the fact that it is almost impossible to convey tone, attitude, vocal inflections, and facial expressions in an e-mail the same way you can in person.

"I can't talk. I'm in an e-mail mood."

E-mail

E-mail is one of the largest causes of communication breakdowns. It is fast, easy, and gets our message out there, but it does not take into account the emotions that can be read in the message. Building rapport is the ultimate goal of communication, and an e-mail can ruin that rapport with the click of a mouse.

Many studies have been conducted regarding the likelihood of conflict and e-mail messaging. Kristin Byron, from Syracuse University's business school, finds that conflict and miscommunication with e-mail is likely. The intent of the sender isn't always clear, and positive e-mail messages may be interpreted as more neutral, and neutral e-mails as more negative. She found jokes were rated as less funny by recipients than by senders.

On the Side

"Recently I was in a negotiation to sell my company for a substantial amount of money. The prospective buyer asked me to e-mail my expectations for the buyout. I proceeded to be as direct as I could and wrote down everything I expected. After reading the e-mail a couple of times, I sent it. I then called the prospective buyer after sending the e-mail, and they were furious. They had read many additional messages into my e-mail that I thought were harmless. Needless to say, the deal didn't go through."

—Owner of a privately owned printing company

Other factors that can harm overall communication when e-mailing is the look of the e-mail, how formal or informal it is, and whether it contains spelling errors. A typo or a misplaced word can cause the recipient to question the professionalism of the sender. E-mail is a wonderful mode of communication when used in the correct way for the correct purpose. When you are trying to build or strengthen a relationship, pick up the telephone or walk to the other person's office instead. This will ensure that they are receiving the intended message.

Best Practices for E-Mail

» Make sure the subject line is pertinent and to the point.

» Write an e-mail like a letter, with a greeting, body, and closing.

» Do not use color or design as a background for a professional e-mail.

» Use punctuation correctly.

» Reread the e-mail slowly to ensure that there are no errors.

» Remember that spell check does not catch incorrect word usage, just misspelled words.

» Be direct and to the point. Most people do not have time to read long e-mails.

» If the e-mail has to have all of the details, put the executive summary at the top, outline what the e-mail includes, and then provide the details.

» If you would like to add an e-mail disclaimer like "sensitive" or "do not forward," place it in the subject line. Be aware that people often glance at e-mails and do not read all the way to the end, which is why the disclaimer should be put in the subject line.

DO send an e-mail:

» When you are relaying information with no emotional attachment.

» When you need to give a concise response.

» With less frequency than physical or telephone contact; make sure more direct contact is used with a 3:1 ratio to e-mail. Face-to-face and telephone contact builds relationships. E-mail does not.

Do NOT send an e-mail:

» If the topic is emotional. Pick up the telephone or make an appointment to resolve the issue.

➠ If the other person becomes emotional during the e-mail exchange, pick up the phone.

➠ If the e-mail exchange is going back and forth with no resolution, pick up the phone and bring closure to the conversation.

➠ If the e-mail sounds the least bit emotional, or if you are not sure, have someone objective read it.

➠ When you are angry or upset, do not ever put your feelings in writing.

➠ To your entire address book. Send an e-mail only to the necessary parties.

➠ If it is a direct and lengthy response to only one person.

On the Side

"An e-mail came and there were three typos. I could tell that it was sent quickly and in response to a question. Unfortunately, the e-mail had been forwarded to two internal colleagues and external customers. When I was with one of the external customers, they made a comment to me about the e-mail, saying, 'Do you think that Dave is the right person for this project?' When I asked why they would say that, the customer mentioned the typos in the e-mail and stressed that the details were what made his company successful."

—Director of a PR firm

➠ If you risk projecting an image to your superiors that your day is spent mostly sending and reading e-mail, thus making them wonder what else you should be doing.

➠ If you do not wish to have it forwarded to others.

Ask Yourself These Crucial Questions About E-mail

➠ What message am I trying to send?

➠ Have I reread this e-mail enough times to catch any errors?

➠ Should I call or make an appointment with the person instead?

Texting

Texting can lead to all kinds of social faux pas and misunderstandings, so keep the following ideas in mind before you press "send." Also, keep in mind this one caveat: Know your customer, know your colleague. This is changing as the pace of business keeps increasing and additional generations enter the workforce. Adapt to the receiver to meet your goals.

▶ The biggest offense is texting while having a face-to-face conversation.

▶ Focus on the person in front of you.

▶ Just because your colleagues are texting does not mean that it is professional; look for ways to set yourself apart.

▶ Know when it is appropriate to use shorthand and emoticons.

▶ Texting should be your last alternative when communicating with a customer unless that is how they like to communicate. Keep track and document all of the texts sent back and forth.

▶ Take the customer's lead with texting but realize that it does not ever take the place of a real conversation.

Ask Yourself These Crucial Questions About Texting

▶ What message am I trying to send?

▶ Does this message match my professionalism? Is it too casual?

▶ Should I call the person instead?

Bonus Tips for E-mail and Texting

Another thing to consider when sending texts or e-mails to a professional contact is response time. Understanding the importance of this small detail can go a long way with current or future clients.

▶ Know the expectation of your key stakeholders. We have many clients who feel that two hours is too long to get a response for any e-mail or text that is sent.

▶ Each company has its own standards and each manager may have his or her own standards. The key is to manage expectations.

▶ The general rule of thumb is no more than three hours to at least acknowledge that you have received the message.

Also, people do not realize how others interpret their e-mails. Researchers find that the sender of an e-mail writes from his or her perspective and assumes that the recipient will read the message with the same perspective. In fact, it is hard for the sender to realize that his or her intention will be interpreted in any other way than what he or she meant.

Over the years multiple e-mail experiments have been conducted to see how closely aligned the sender's message is to the recipient's understanding of the communication. In 2005, *The Journal of Personality and Social Psychology* published an article called "Egocentrism Over E-Mail: Can We Communicate as Well as We Think?" Justin Kruger of New York University, Nicholas Epley of the University of Illinois at Urbana–Champaign, and Jason Parker and Zhi-Wen Ng of Stein School of Business at NYU conducted five experiments. The results showed that even when senders tried to put themselves into the receivers' shoes and take on the receivers' perspectives, they were not able to move far away from their own perspectives. This led to the inability to convey humor, tone, and other emotions. Through these studies, they realized that most people do not have an awareness of how their messages will be understood even when they were trying to adapt, resulting in communication breakdowns and unclear messages.

(For additional and more in-depth tips on technology protocol, read *You Did What? The Biggest Blunders Professionals Make.*)

Big Mistake 8 \ Not Managing Your Social Networking

Don't say anything online that you wouldn't want plastered on a billboard with your face on it.

—Erin Bury

Social media is an extension of your brand. Be smart, realize that nothing is private, and know that what you post can be used in a court of law. On the flip side, if social media is used well, it is an effective way to make connections with business associates. Keep in mind that everything you put online will be there forever. This can affect your professional life, no matter your age when you posted something or how long ago you posted it.

"Right, like the boss will know I'm spending all day schmoozing on Facebook."

Together with social media gurus Lauren Feinstein and Adam Tobolowsky, we have compiled best practices advice for integrating social media into your business plan. This chapter focuses on building your personal and professional brand through your social media.

Many are apprehensive when approaching social media. They fear diving into something they possibly could not sustain. The importance of social media can be based only on how much work the user puts into it. Imagine an individual consumer seeking a specific product using only social media. That person would use search terms specific to his or her needs and choose the most credible-looking account to make the purchase. A social media account that has been built, but not maintained, will more times than not get dropped for something more up-to-date. The viral nature of social media is undeniable and has recently been responsible for the worldwide uprisings and changing of political regimes, yet people are still timid when using it to market their business. The power of social media is vast, and with the correct tools, *you can succeed!*

On the Side

"Our recruiting team checks Facebook and other social media outlets for applicants. People are out of control with what they post. I recommend people ask themselves if they ever plan on being in business. If the answer is yes, then stay away. There is a reason that FBI agents and most law enforcement officials don't use Facebook personally—it can put too much in the open that people with bad intentions can use. The same goes for work."

—Partner of a consulting firm

As stated on LinkedIn.com, there are two advantages of social media: First, it is instant. You can quickly respond to customer demands and feedback. Second, you can use your site to speak to other businesses and increase online traffic back to your own business.

On the other hand, there are a couple of disadvantages of social media: It's time-consuming. Keeping your online presence and content up-to-date requires time. Also, unhappy customers can post feedback instantly—and to a much wider audience.

It is important to manage both the positive and negative aspects of social media. Most importantly, you must manage it as you are communicating through everything you write online.

LinkedIn

By using the tools LinkedIn provides, you will be able to efficiently connect, organize, and even reconnect with past, current, and future networks. For example, when asked to specify "How do you know this person," fill in the content diligently to categorize and retain contacts over years of experience. When the time comes, you will be prepared. Keep in mind that LinkedIn is a virtual résumé and networking site that is strictly for business use. It is a professional/social networking site as opposed to a social/social networking site.

Best Practices for LinkedIn

▶ Keep your updates business related.

▶ Your professional credibility can be put at stake by any questionable or politically incorrect postings.

▶ Postings should be less frequent, putting more emphasis on professional quality rather than quantity.

▶ Groups can be used to expand your personal and professional brand. Joining groups and exposing yourself to new potential contacts that have the same professional interests as you will enable you to present your thoughts to unique eyes.

▶ An insightful comment can go a long way. This is an important tool for any professional making new connections through current connections.

- Make sure your page is well written and well thought out.

- Proofread for errors, keep your information clear, and be concise (people want the bottom line).

- LinkedIn is a tool for the entry-level employee all the way up to the CEO.

- On the ground level, sourcing is made easier for those account managers seeking a decision-maker. On the other end, a CEO can manage his expansive list of contacts as well as present a demonstrative leadership persona to others.

On the Side

"I can't believe how many college students put inappropriate photos of themselves online. Do they not realize that recruiters look up everyone on social media these days? We have not hired many people due to inappropiate postings."

—Recruiter for a Fortune 500 company

Facebook

There are two types of Facebook accounts: personal pages and business pages. This means you should not have two personal pages and use one for professional use and the other for friends and family. It is vital to use the appropriate kind of account for the topic at hand. If the account is to keep up with friends and family, create a personal page; for a business, use a business page. You are not beating the system by not following this protocol; in fact, not using the right page could hurt your efforts to reach a wider market. When promoting a brand, splitting resources in half hurts the overall goal; that is, having two Facebook pages promoting the same brand splits the amount of likes the brand will get. Unfortunately, most people don't have the attention span to "like" the same thing twice. Focus your efforts on *one* page and start stockpiling fans.

Best Practices for Facebook

▶ Use appropriate privacy settings, but don't be too trusting. Somebody (employer, family, even law enforcement) seeking to find information about you can always succeed, even with a strict privacy setting.

▶ Where there is a will, there is a way to find someone on the Internet. Be cautious.

▶ It's best to develop a custom privacy setting for both your personal and business pages, as both are different in nature and content; therefore, they deserve different attention and management.

▶ Privacy settings are no longer simply restricted to photos, messages, and friend requests. Facebook has innovated to the level of specifying between friends, acquaintances, family, and others. This allows for the appropriate content to be published to the appropriate audiences and hides the content from others and those who need not view those posts.

▶ Do not post anything negative about work. Be aware that many employers *do* track Internet usage on company computers.

▶ Be sensitive to the amount of posts you write. People do not like having their feeds clogged with unnecessary information. This will compel others to unfriend or unlike your account and ruin a professional or personal relationship.

On the Side

"I couldn't believe it when one of my clients wrote how much she hated work that week and was ready for Friday. The real issue was that all of her colleagues were reading the same thing. What was she thinking? People who make those mistakes are lucky to have a job. I would never promote someone who wrote that."

—Manager at an IT outsourcing company

 Three Facebook posts a day is a good amount for a personal account, unless you have developed into an industry thought leader. In that case, make sure to accommodate Facebook posting supply and demand.

YouTube

With billions and billions in traffic, YouTube has become one of the Internet's top sources for visual knowledge. Many brands, companies, products, and services are viewed on You-Tube daily, creating newfound revenue. If you're a do-it-yourself or how-to person, YouTube is a must. YouTube value plays a vital roll in your overall Internet presence and is a stepping stone that must be in place.

Best Practices for YouTube

 Before you jump in and make videos, make sure you understand the terms of service.

 Keep up with comments on your videos.

 Use this platform as another way to make new relationships.

 Your YouTube channel design adds legitimacy and therefore should be planned out before you upload the first video.

 Making sure your video formatting is in spec with YouTube requirements will result in more views and quicker growth.

Twitter

Twitter differs from other platforms in terms of content; it's more about *what* is said than of *who* said it. Searches are more keyword based, whereas searches on Facebook focus more on people. If your Twitter handle is used under a pseudonym and content doesn't identify back to you, feel free to be silly and have fun. If your Twitter represents you personally or professionally, filter your thoughts. Twitter gives people a powerful voice and should not be abused. Everything you write on Twitter is public; be careful that you are communicating your brand.

Best Practices for Twitter

▶ Be witty and expressive, but be aware that being heard can lead to problems if not executed properly.

▶ Be mindful that despite the decision to delete a post, people still could have seen it in the brief time it was published. Certain programs allow others to see posts even if deleted, especially if they include profanity.

▶ Use Twitter as a tool to express insight into your industry.

▶ Being active in the online community of your interest gives the ability to become a thought leader. Insightful comments provide a basis for industry credibility and mass exposure as a public figure or as a business leader.

▶ Follow those who interest you; this will broaden your horizons, which ultimately leads to new followers. Followers equal power and leverage.

▶ If the goal is raising awareness, every follower represents a vast new network of potential viewers, which emphasizes the viral nature of Twitter and social media as a whole.

▶ Utilize the search box with subjects of interest and find new conversations to join and others to follow.

▶ Consider following people suggested by Twitter, and take note in trending topics.

▶ Use a business Twitter account to create business relationships.

▶ Teach your clients how to follow you and then make sure you keep your tweets professional.

▶ Be conversational. Use Twitter as a discussion forum; it enables your clients to see that others respect you, too.

▶ Thank people when they make comments.

▶ Do not be an overposter; this will make you lose followers. It is important to understand that Twitter allows 140 characters for a reason. People on Twitter are looking for and expecting the bottom line.

Blogging

Anything you blog regarding work can be used against you, so use your professional voice rather than slang. Also, edit your posts and make sure there are no typos or grammatical errors. Be clear and concise. As we've mentioned with other social media outlets, don't be too personal; keep your opinions to yourself. Make your blog personable, interesting, informative, and useful for readers so they will keep coming back.

Best Practices for Blogging

▶ Do not post anything negative about work where colleagues or customers can read it. Manage your settings well and make your information private to the public.

▶ Be aware that many employers can track Internet usage on company computers.

▶ The wrong message can drive people away from your brand.

On the Side

"I can't believe how employees of this company put inappropriate comments online. Do they not realize that what they post affects how I see them based on the choices they make outside of work? They should keep it private; I really don't want to know what they do."

—VP of human resources, national skin care company

Ask Yourself These Crucial Questions

▶ Have I figured out the ROI on building my online presence?

▶ Am I committed to spending at least one hour a week to build my online brand?

Big Mistake 9 ⟩ Lack of Awareness of Communication Stallers and Stoppers

> *What is necessary to change a person is to change his awareness of himself.*
>
> —Abraham Maslow

Have you ever heard of stallers and stoppers in business? Stallers and stoppers are characteristics or behaviors that can stall or stop his or her career. In two decades we have trained and worked with more than 100,000 people. In many of our sessions we ask participants what behaviors make them "shut down" to the point at which they do not want to work with the other person. This chapter focuses on the top answers we repeatedly hear.

"The negotiations were going great until Kruger decided to 'Go Negative.'"

Negativity in the workplace is toxic and should be managed. However, individuals often don't know they are being negative. After interviewing 100 of our clients specifically about how they "hear" negativity from their colleagues, we chose some of the statements that they interpreted as negative and examples of how these statements could become positive. As you read the adjacent chart, think about what you say and how it could be interpreted.

Other Communication Stallers

Interrupting

"If a is success in life, then a equals x plus y plus z. Work is x; y is play; and z is keeping your mouth shut."

—Albert Einstein

When we ask people what behavior drives them crazy, interrupting is one of the most common answers. Interrupting can halt all communication. It makes other people

Negative Statement	Positive Turnaround
I can't do that.	I can do that.
I don't know what you're referring to.	Help me understand what you're referring to.
I don't think that happened.	Remind me of what took place.
I can't take it.	I will handle this.
I knew this would happen to me.	I am prepared to navigate this change.
I don't know what the real issues is here.	Let's agree on the real issue.
I didn't do it.	We need to create a solution.
It is so annoying when people ask stupid questions.	I am happy to answer any questions.
She always does that.	I see a pattern in what she is doing.
He never does that.	I would like to see more of...
This is so unfair.	So where are we?
I can't believe this place.	It is an interesting place.
He is so obnoxious.	He is unique.

think that you do not care about what they are saying. In turn, when a person interrupts, they have the ability to halt opportunities and the chance to build relationships. There is nothing worse than trying to say something and someone else either finishes your sentence or interrupts you with something they think is more important.

On the Side

"One of my best sales associates asked me for a raise. He does a tremendous job, but he always interrupts when I am speaking. Or worse yet, he finishes my sentences. When I sat down to tell him that he deserved the raise because he had exceeded his goals, he interrupted me and said that he was disappointed that I couldn't give him a raise, but he understood. If he had just let me finish, I think he would have liked my outcome a lot more than his."

—Sales manager at a home improvement store

Best Practices

▶ Never assume what someone is going to tell you.

▶ Approach every conversation with the thought that you are going to learn something new.

▶ Focus on what the person is saying, not on what you are going to say next.

▶ If you like to give advice, stop thinking about what you are going to say and make sure that the person actually wants advice and is not just venting.

▶ When the person stops talking, wait three seconds to make sure they really are finished.

▶ Many times a customer is telling you exactly how they want you to sell them, and if you are listening, you will know how to close the deal.

▶ Do not interrupt other people in meetings; it's a bad reflection on you.

On the Side

"I have a terrible habit of interrupting. I was with one of my colleagues, and while we were walking in to a meeting, she was telling me a story. I thought that I knew how she was feeling and what she was about to say. Every time she couldn't think of the word she was trying to capture, I finished her sentence. Finally, she said to me, 'Do you think you could just let me finish a thought and tell you how I feel?' I was taken aback, to say the least, but after thinking about it, I realized how rude I had been. I now make a very conscious effort not to finish sentences or interrupt."

—Pharmaceutical sales representative

Ask Yourself These Crucial Questions

▶ How do I feel when someone interrupts me?

▶ When someone else is speaking, am I listening or am I waiting anxiously to start speaking?

▶ Do I wait until someone has finished speaking before I join the conversation?

Talking Too Much

"The less said, the better."

—Jane Austen

Good conversation should never be misinterpreted as good communication. When someone asks a direct question, generally they are looking for a concise and direct answer. In the business arena, it is important to stay focused on the business at hand and not to be overly communicative about issues that have no bearing. Even in social settings, when people talk too much, other people cannot get out of the conversation quickly enough.

On the Side

"I interviewed an extremely sharp young man for a sales position. He held himself well, his body language was positive—we were off to a good start. I asked him to tell me what he was looking for in a career. When I looked down at my watch, it was 30 minutes later and he was still going. There was no stopping in sight. No matter what position we're in, it is so important to know when we've oversold. Knowing how to be concise, yet informative, is crucial to communication success."

—VP of sales for an automotive group

Best Practices

➧ Always be interested, not interesting. You will always seem more interesting when you are interested in the other person.

➧ If the other person keeps looking away, you are probably not holding their attention.

➧ When you start to notice glazed-over eyes with no reaction to what you are saying, *stop* talking.

➧ If the other person has not said anything for at least five minutes, they might be thinking about other things.

➧ Focus on the other person's body language. If they are not looking at you, nodding, or leaning forward, you have lost them.

➧ Keep personal conversations to a minimum unless in an appropriate environment.

➧ Keep personal information to a minimum.

Ask Yourself These Crucial Questions

➧ Has the other person said anything in the last five minutes?

➧ Am I being as interested as I am interesting?

➧ How do I get back on track when I realize I have gone off on a tangent that is of no interest to the other person?

Being a Know-It-All

"People don't care how much you know until they
know how much you care."

—Theodore Roosevelt

There is a difference between knowing a lot and being a
"know-it-all." How do you know if you are a know-it-all? Have
people ever referred to you as a "smart aleck"? If you know
everything about everything at all times—or so you think—you
may be one of these people. Remember the Johari Window? It
is time to get feedback from someone you trust. Being so smart
all the time is actually holding you back. No one wants to be
with a know-it-all; it's draining, and most of us stop listening.
You cannot reach your communication goal if people are not
hearing what you have to say.

Best Practices

> Remember that there is a time and a place to share what
you know.

> Be a listener.

> Take notice of whether or not people are asking you to con-
tribute to the conversation.

> Ask questions.

> Find a mentor who can help you learn to listen and practice
empathy.

> Stop letting your ego get in the way.

Ask Yourself These Crucial Questions

> Do my friends and family joke that I am a know-it-all?

> Do I find myself taking up more than 80 percent of most con-
versations? How can I make that no more than 50 percent?

> When do I have the opportunity to practice changing my
behavior?

Being Unfocused or Not Paying Full Attention

"I think the one lesson I have learned is that there is no substitute for paying attention."

—Diane Sawyer

No one wants to be discounted. When we do not focus on the other person, we are not only discounting them, we are also making a very crucial communication mistake. When we do not focus on the conversation at hand, we destroy trust. When we are fully present when communicating, we build trust. It starts at a handshake. When shaking someone's hand and using direct eye contact, you build immediate rapport. On the flip side, when you are distracted and looking around, the other person feels discounted. Staying focused is a communication and rapport-building skill that can build long-term relationships.

Valerie Jarrett plays a lot of roles. She is the president's closest personal adviser, the first couple's friend, and the chief liaison for the White House. Through the years, Jarrett has given their nonsupporters the cold shoulder; however, she has realized that this may not be the best course of action for changing opinions. Jarrett actually made an announcement to an audience at the White House that they have to be better

On the Side

"We conducted a management survey, and the participants were going around the room talking about what they respected most about their own managers. One up-and-coming manager said that the one thing that she respected most about her manager was that every time she walked into her office, no matter what her manager was doing, her manager stopped and focused on her. It made her feel important and of value to the team. It also was teaching her how to be a better leader."

—Hospital supervisor

messengers and that the administration was now open to any and all conversations and comments.

Jarrett's message is poignant: no matter who you are and whether or not you agree with the person talking, being open and engaged increases your communication effectiveness.

Best Practices
On the Telephone/Cell Phone
- Stand up, turn away from your desk, and focus on the conversation.
- If it is necessary to take notes, do not start doodling; stay focused.
- Do not start working on other things; the person on the other end will be able to tell.
- Stay engaged or end the conversation before you end a good business relationship.

Meetings
- Put down everything and focus.
- Have a pen in your hand only if you are taking notes on the current conversation.
- Do not use your phone; put it on "do not disturb."
- Close the door if necessary and do not allow any interruptions.
- Go into a private conference room if necessary.
- Make eye contact.
- Do not have sidebar conversations with your neighbors.
- Do not make eye contact that could be perceived as negative to other meeting participants.
- Keep your body language engaged; do not start fidgeting.
- Stay focused on the conversation or agenda.
- The more respect you give to other people, the more respect you will receive.

> ## On the Side
> "I am so busy all of the time. When people come to me with their issues, I have a hard time concentrating on what they need me to do because I have a number of to-do's on my own list. I realized that I was forgetting things, not focusing on my employees, and losing the respect of my colleagues. I started carrying around a small notebook and now anytime anyone asks me to do something, I write it down. My coworkers know that I am paying attention to them and listening. It also ensures that I do what I say I'll do without having to keep everything in my memory."
>
> —National accounts manager, luxury goods

Networking

➧ When shaking hands, make direct eye contact.

➧ Listen and focus on names so that you can use them and introduce others if necessary.

➧ Do not look over someone's shoulder to see who else is there.

➧ When there are many people in the conversation, don't have side conversations with one or two people in the group.

➧ Follow through on what you promise; this will let others know that you are reliable and were listening to them.

Ask Yourself These Crucial Questions

➧ When I am trying to get someone's attention and they do not stop what they are doing, how does that make me feel?

➧ When someone is talking to me, do I stop everything else I am doing to focus on the person? If not, what effect do I think that has on our relationship?

➧ What are some things I can do that will make every person I am speaking to feel valued?

Being Defensive

"When angry, count ten before you speak; if very angry, a hundred."

—Thomas Jefferson

Have you ever felt your blood pressure rise when someone said or did something to annoy you? Or when someone confronted you about something you did? Defensive behavior usually surfaces in situations where conflict, pressure, or threats are present. Usually a red flag goes up in our minds when we feel attacked, manipulated, judged, or reprimanded.

Generally our ability to think clearly and be rational is compromised while in a defensive behavior mode. It is so easy to react. The hard part is thinking about how your reaction can affect your credibility.

Always take the high road, even when someone puts you on the defensive. This behavior will command respect. Remember that many times their intention is to tell you how they are feeling. If you are on your A-game, you will ask yourself, "What can I learn from what they are telling me? How can I grow from this?" We make mistakes when we think we can't grow from a situation and are more concerned about our ego than the real message.

On the Side

"I ran a meeting last week and my colleague came up to me and said, 'I have a great opportunity for you.' I was immediately excited. Then she said, 'When you are running meetings, I want you to be aware of the number of um's you use and how you repeat sentences when you're not sure what to say.' Well, that was not the opportunity I expected. I immediately began to make excuses. Being self-aware, I then realized that she supports me 100 percent and was only telling me this to grow."

—Financial advisor

Best Practices

❯ Become more self-aware.

❯ Know what your hot buttons are.

❯ Try not to react or be overwhelmed; breathe.

❯ Realize that you can walk away, think about what has just been said, and deal with it later when you are more rational.

❯ Stop and say, "I hear what you are saying." This allows the other person to feel heard.

❯ Use clarifying statements, such as: "Let me see if I understand you correctly…" or "I want to make sure I am hearing what you're saying…"

❯ Don't keep talking and telling; ask questions to gain clarity.

❯ Let your ego go; it's all right not to have the last word.

❯ React in a way that commands respect and credibility.

Ask Yourself These Crucial Questions

❯ How do I react when I hear things I disagree with or have a different opinion about?

❯ What do I do when I read someone else's defensive behavior?

❯ How can I communicate while I am feeling defensive?

Words That Detract

Have you ever been in a situation where someone used inappropriate words, dialect, examples, or stories, and you just wanted to cringe? Unfortunately these things can stick with us and may affect how we perceive working with that person.

We have all done this. Sometimes we don't even realize what we are doing or saying. Based on the listener's experiences and education, our words can speak volumes.

Some terms have actually become acceptable words because of high usage. The bottom line is that people who know the appropriate usage know when a word is being misused, and it can affect their perceptions.

The following table provides some examples of words or pronunciations that are incorrect, as well as more appropriate words to use instead.

One Step Back	One Step Ahead
Gonna	Going to
Wanna	Want to
Irregardless	Regardless
Etiqwett	Etiquette
Gimme	Give me
Totally	Absolutely
Aks	Ask
Yous guys	All of you
Yeah	Yes
No problem	Of course
Overused words: Okay Really You know	Replacements for overused words: Pause Listen Nod
Vulgarity and curse words	Eliminate all vulgarity and curse words from your vocabulary.
I'm doing good	I'm doing well

On the Side

"Have you ever heard yourself using a certain word and immediately felt like it made you seem less professional or uneducated? I had to cringe during a meeting when I responded to a VP with the word 'totally' and they asked me if I was a Valley girl. Another time I used the word 'okay' repeatedly and someone commented on how annoying it was to hear the word over and over again. A few other times I have felt uncomfortable when I say things like 'expecially' instead of 'especially' or 'error on the side of caution' instead of 'err on the side of caution.' I realized how important it is to use proper grammar and avoid slang and casual words because I could see how people perceived me."

—Insurance company project manager

Best Practices

▶ Ask a mentor or friend what words they notice you use a lot.

▶ If people say things like, "That's your word," take a hint.

▶ Record yourself when doing a presentation or leading a meeting.

▶ Pause; become comfortable with quiet gaps.

▶ Use nonverbal gestures.

▶ Read more and become acquainted with new words.

▶ When you don't understand the meaning of a word, look it up.

▶ Ask yourself if certain pronunciations you grew up with are holding you back in your professional life.

Ask Yourself These Crucial Questions

▶ What are my comfort words when I am filling gaps of quiet space?

▶ What words do I overuse? If I don't know, who can I ask?

▶ How do I eliminate these words?

Filler Words When Presenting

Have you ever attended a presentation where you knew the presenter and were astounded by how a seemingly articulate person cracked under pressure? The colleague who speaks clearly and is respected by his or her team members stammers and stutters, and interjects "um" and "uh" in every other sentence. Why does this happen?

There are many "filler" words in English for when we don't know how to continue in a sentence, such as "hmmm," "er," and "like."

In general, when speakers say these filler words or perform filler actions (such as licking their lips), they do so subconsciously. They make these sounds or do these actions at a transition point when they are getting ready to move on to another topic or offer an example. The simple act of switching from one topic to another demands a transition, and when one has not been determined by the speaker beforehand, the subconscious fills in. So, for some, it is a less-than-articulate "uh," and for others, it is scratching the head. In either case, the behavior can be stopped.

The best way to eliminate filler words and actions is to substitute one behavior for another. So, at points of transition or whenever you feel the need to inject a filler, simply *pause*. Take a deep breath and gather your thoughts. The pause that seems so long to you is actually a welcome respite for your audience. They, too, need a break in order to concentrate.

Ask Yourself These Crucial Questions

➡ What slang or filler words do I use over and over again?

➡ When other people speak, what do I notice?

➡ What can I do to eliminate fillers and casual words from my professional life?

Big Mistake 10 ⟩ Making Assumptions

We are all faced with a series of great opportunities brilliantly disguised as impossible situations.

—Charles R. Swindoll

Many things can get in our way when it comes to communication. We can let these things bog us down or we can deal with them in order to improve our situation and our relationships. Poor business communication can prevent career growth.

Assumptions

In his book *Overcoming Organizational Defenses*, Chris Argyris discusses the Ladder of Inference, a model that explains our thinking process. We all have experiences in our head, and when we process events that happen, we go through a series of steps to reach a conclusion based on what we have already experienced and then we act accordingly.

In other words, we have information coming in and, based on our observations, we select what we think is appropriate for the situation, we analyze it, and we take action.

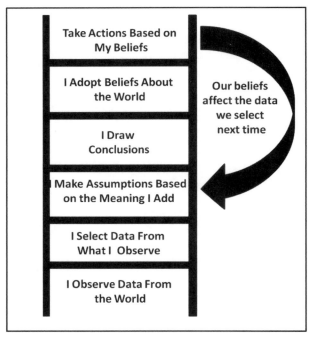

Reprinted from Peter Senge, *The Fifth Discipline Fieldbook.*

Here is the problem: All of this happens very quickly, and what seems to be clear in our own minds might be obvious only to us. We select what catches our attention and we dismiss what we don't want to see. We add meaning to what we do see; hence we make assumptions and draw conclusions based on those assumptions.

All of this is happening when we're communicating. In simple terms, we all bring our own set of past experiences and baggage to every interaction. We draw conclusions as to why someone is acting in a certain way and we naturally assume that their motivations, behaviors, wants, desires, likes, and dislikes should match our own. Then, our emotions kick in and we start reacting, either positively or negatively. In a work situation, this is where we respond based on our conclusions, and it is often emotional rather than rational. The cycle continues and this happens all day long.

The following example can give you a better idea of what we are talking about here. I had an employee who was generally a great employee. However, for the last two months he had not been thorough when documenting his work. When I looked for a piece of client information that should have been documented, it wasn't there. "Of course," I thought. "He never documents." My immediate assumptions included: he's lazy, he doesn't follow through, he doesn't do what I ask, he may not be right for the job, and he expects a lot but doesn't do his part.

Based on the interpreted facts and my assumptions, my conclusions were that I had lost respect for this employee. My belief is that what you put into work you get out. My actions, based on my beliefs, told me that I needed to reprimand my employee. I started to go through the Ladder of Inference in my mind.

Initially, I did not think about what could be going on with this employee, such as:

- ▶ The employee has been struggling at work and was embarrassed to ask for help.

- ▶ The documentation is there, but it was in the wrong place.

- ▶ I made an error in looking it up.

- ▶ He is overwhelmed and can't keep up.

- ▶ There is a system glitch and he didn't realize it.

- ▶ He is not the right person for the job.

Due to my awareness that I might be perceiving this incorrectly, I thought about handling the conversation very differently. There were a couple possible solutions:

- ▶ "Can you help me understand why the documentation is missing?"

▶ "I know that this isn't typical for you, but for the last two months, I haven't seen any documentation. Can you tell me what's going on? Help me understand."

It is important to start with the awareness that this is taking place. Then we have to change behavior in order to not make mistakes that can cost us a relationship.

Best Practices

▶ Be aware of how your assumptions can affect your communication.

▶ Try to understand the root of your feelings.

▶ Try to be transparent and let the other person know where you are coming from based on your assumptions, interpretations, and conclusions without being defensive.

▶ Allow others to test your assumptions without being condescending.

▶ Use open-ended and nonjudgmental questions rather than questions that exhibit a bias.

▶ Don't agree or disagree too soon.

▶ Be respectful.

Ask Yourself These Crucial Questions

▶ Past experiences are good predictors. Reflecting on past opportunities, what could I do differently in the future?

▶ Am I looking at all of my solutions?

▶ What attitude am I choosing when confronted with roadblocks?

Is the Story Fact or Fiction?

"He didn't include me in that meeting for a reason." "Did you see her roll her eyes?" "I know he was talking about me after that meeting." "They don't like me."

Have you thought or said anything like this before? Without getting into the science of our brains, let's discuss how thinking or saying these statements are stallers and stoppers to effective communication.

It is important to realize that when we feel negative about a situation, we communicate that through our behavior without even saying a word. It is also communicated through the words we use with others regarding the situation.

First, where do these thoughts come from and how do they materialize into stories in our minds? Embellished stories are built in our minds based on our perception of another person's actions, as well as our own feelings about ourselves at any given time. These stories can spiral into unnecessary drama, which ultimately causes a breakdown in communication and the relationship. Imagine a fan in your head blowing all of the stories around. The more we read into behavior, the stronger the fan blows.

The outcome of these stories in your minds can ultimately stall your career. The key is to know what is emotional and what is real. Sometimes it is hard to tell the difference. During these times, here are some questions to help you navigate through the emotion and slow down the "fan" enough to evaluate the validity of your thoughts:

- ▶ What are the actual facts of the situation without any emotion attached?
- ▶ Is this real?
- ▶ Am I making this up?
- ▶ How would this be viewed if I were seeing this happen to someone else?
- ▶ What am I missing?
- ▶ Am I feeling bad about myself right now? Or about my actions leading to this?

▶ Is there something in my past that is making me overgeneralize what is happening?

▶ Can I confide in someone who will stay unemotional and help me navigate this situation?

Sometimes we create drama in our personal and professional lives based on a variety of factors. It is our obligation to stop creating the fiction and seek more facts. This can build your career and your relationships as opposed to stalling or stopping them.

Automatic Negative Thoughts (ANT) is an acronym that can help you deal with the stories in your mind. We have ANTs every day and in many situations. The more awareness we have, the easier it will be to squash the ANTs and turn any situation into something positive. Look at the following example to understand how you can integrate this technique into your daily thoughts.

ANT: I wasn't included in Jesse's meeting. She doesn't like me.

Anti ANT: I am glad that I didn't have to go to that meeting. I have so much going on this week. I bet it didn't have to do with my area of expertise.

ANT: He rolled his eyes during my presentation. Was he bored? Does he not like me?

Anti ANT: I hope he's okay. He must have a lot going on in his mind. He usually isn't like that. Maybe I should check in with him to find out what is going on with him.

It is critical to our success that we do not let these stallers or stoppers get in the way of how we communicate. Take time to reflect before jumping into an assumption. Ask the right questions. Seek to understand. Keep your goal in mind and the drama away.

Big Mistake 11 \ Not Focusing on the Details

Beware of the person who can't be bothered by details.

—William Feather

The details matter. Dotting your i's and crossing your t's does make a difference. Why is it that you focus on a spot on someone's shirt rather than on what they are saying? Why is it that when someone gives you a limp handshake, you focus on the handshake and not on the skills they bring to the table? If someone misspells your name, you start checking for other mistakes. As we have discussed throughout the book, we communicate through our actions. These actions communicate our brand and what people can expect from us. These expectations come from the details in our daily behaviors.

Keep your eye on the big picture. Although it is important to be aware of potential opportunities and threats as well as determine the direction that you will take, it does not mean that you can afford to neglect the details. Many times it is the little things that make the difference between a person who is successful and one who is not.

> ## On the Side
> "Recently I was planning a large client event and we had chosen a specific caterer. I couldn't believe it when the proposal came and our company name was misspelled. When I said something, the person didn't apologize but told me they were so busy and that's why it was misspelled. I didn't want to hear an excuse, just an apology."
>
> —Events director for a hedge fund

Best Practices

Tracking and Following Up

➧ Keep track of conversations and keep your notes in one location.

➧ Follow up when you say you will.

➧ Set reminders.

➧ Follow up even if you don't know the final status.

➧ Think ahead. Think about the implications of an interaction and the reason for follow-up. If there are others that need to be involved, notify them. Also keep abreast of potential risks.

➧ If you don't have a good tracking system, implement and utilize one. There are many out there, such as ACT, Daylite, Salesforce.com, Outlook, and others.

➧ Be meticulous about keeping everything together.

Handwritten Notes

➧ Make sure your note has no mistakes, including no crossed-out words.

➧ A handwritten note should be exactly that, not an e-mail.

➧ Use a pen.

➧ Send a note preferably within three days of the event; if you forget and it is late, write it anyway and start with, "I am so sorry that it has taken me so long to thank you…"

▶ Write handwritten notes when you meet a new person, a client gives you new business, or someone helps you do, get, or accomplish something.

▶ Send a note when there is an occasion or congratulations are in order, such as a promotion.

▶ Write a note when you want to be at the top of someone's mind or just to say hello.

▶ Write a note if you want to show that you are grateful to a colleague.

On the Side

"It was not a coincidence when I wrote a note to a client just to say hi and two days later she called to discuss a project for which they wanted to hire us."

—Designer with an architecture firm

Ask Yourself These Crucial Questions

▶ Have I taken the time to thank the people I work with on a regular basis?

▶ How will I ensure that I check the details of my work?

▶ Do I follow up when I say I will? How do I stay on top of my schedule and my to-do's?

Not Giving and Receiving Precise Feedback

Feedback is the breakfast of champions.

—Ken Blanchard

Feedback is critical to a person or a team that wants to continue to grow. It offers both the sender and the receiver an opportunity to grow. Providing feedback, as well as asking for feedback, is incredibly important and should happen on a regular basis. It can be hard to deliver and receive, and can produce conflict if not planned well or if the receiver is closed-minded. Yet feedback is vital to improving performance and building good relationships.

"My apologies if I was too harsh with you."

In fact, a recent study by Zenger Folkman surveyed 22,719 leaders. Out of those surveyed, 10 percent were rated as not giving honest feedback to their direct reports. The engagement rate from that 10 percent was no higher than 25 percent. In other words, employees who did not get honest feedback were disengaged. From the survey, it was obvious that these employees were not committed to their employers or their jobs. In fact, they would have quit if they could have. Conversely, leaders who were ranked in the top 10 percent for giving honest feedback had employees who were completely engaged. These employees were, at minimum, 77 percent engaged in their jobs *(http://zengerfolkman.com/the-best-gift-leaders-can-give-honest-feedback/)*.

Giving Feedback

The most important thing about feedback is that just giving it is not enough. The information provided needs to be specific, with detailed behavior modification examples. Many people do not know how to change their behavior based on feedback. Thus, we need to give people the "how to's" so that they can modify their behavior.

According to a 2009 Gallup Feedback Study of 1,000 participants:

▶ One in ten supervisors focus on employee weaknesses.

▶ Employees receiving predominantly negative feedback from their managers are 20 times more likely to be engaged than those receiving little or no feedback.

▶ Employees ignored by their manager are twice as likely to be actively disengaged compared with workers whose manager focuses on their weaknesses.

▶ Managers focusing on employee strengths are 30 times more likely to have actively engaged workers compared with managers denying feedback.

▶ Managers focusing on employee strengths are one third more likely to have actively engaged employees compared with managers focusing on weaknesses.

▶ Managers giving little or no feedback to employees result in four out of ten workers being actively disengaged.

▶ Managers giving little or no feedback to their workers fail to engage 98 percent of them.

As you can see, giving little to no feedback on an employee's performance is twice as bad as focusing on the negative. To see the pole online, go to *www.gallup.com/businessjournal/124214/driving-engagement-focusing-strengths.aspx*

Best Practices

▶ Feedback must be specific and focused on an observable behavior: "I noticed when you checked in Mr. Smith..." versus "When you check people in..."

▶ Be timely but not reactive. Watch your tone of voice before you jump right into the feedback.

▶ Feedback must be measurable and achievable. Do not say things like, "I feel like you can try harder." Rather, "When meeting with clients, smile and make eye contact."

▶ Begin with the person's strengths and then go into the areas of development.

▶ There should be no surprises if you are a manager and it is related to the performance of your employees. Feedback should be given early and often.

➧ Ask the recipients of the feedback for their ownership of the issue and their commitment to improvement.

➧ Make sure you let the person know you support *them*, not the behavior.

➧ Criticize the behavior, not the person.

➧ Use clear words, not jargon or vague language.

➧ Listen to the person's comments and do not react with anger or defensiveness.

➧ Summarize the feedback and highlight next steps.

➧ Avoid extreme words like "always" and "never."

➧ Do not compare the person to peers. Discuss their performance and the expectations specifically for them.

➧ Do not apologize for giving feedback.

Here are some suggestions on when (or when not) to give feedback.

When you should give feedback

▶ When the employee has missed a goal and is not identifying the issues on his or her own.

▶ When the employee is not meeting the requirements and expectations you have clearly stated.

▶ When there is information among the employee's peers that may derail his or her career.

▶ When the issue is a performance problem and not merely an irritant.

▶ When the employee is demonstrating behaviors that will be harmful to their career.

When you should *not* give feedback

▶ When it is about your ego and not about enabling the employee to succeed.

▶ When the employee delivers all goals on time and to the defined quality standards.

▶ When there is a lack of supporting data or lack of alignment to the organization's goals.

▶ When you are emotional (for example, angry).

Feedback Conversation Planning

The following questions will help you prepare when you need to provide feedback to others:

▶ What is the communication style of the person receiving the feedback?

▶ What is going to make this person take notice of what you are saying?

▶ What are three points you want to make? (If you cover too many points, you will lose focus.)

▶ What are the benefits to the person if they change the behavior? That is, what's in it for them?

On the Side

"I was sitting in a meeting and my boss completely undermined what I said in front of everyone. She also neglected to mention that I had done the work she presented, and gave herself full credit. She asked for feedback after the meeting. I was committed to making her feel comfortable, yet let her know that her actions affect the team. I was clear and concise and focused on specific actions, not on her as a person. I said, 'During the meeting, I did not receive credit for all of the work I had done. When I made a comment, I felt as though you undermined me when you said that you wouldn't handle the situation that way. My goal is to deliver the best results for this team and a unified relationship. What is your goal?' Fortunately, my boss received the feedback well and we have a much stronger working relationship."

—Customer service agent for a home design firm

▶ What are the risks to both the person and the company if they don't change the behavior?

▶ What questions do you anticipate the person asking as you give feedback?

▶ What solutions and time line can you both come up with during the feedback session?

▶ How will you measure behavioral changes?

Ask Yourself These Crucial Questions

➥ What have I learned from feedback others have given me?

➥ How will I plan out my next feedback session?

➥ How will I receive feedback going forward? What can I learn from this?

Receiving Feedback

You cannot be passive when receiving feedback. Based on the previously mentioned research, you can't rely on consistent feedback from your peers or leaders. It is up to you to get the feedback you need to progress in your career. You cannot grow and develop without understanding how well, or how poorly, you just did on a task.

It has been found that direct and honest feedback and leadership effectiveness are aligned. The Zenger Folkman study that was mentioned at the beginning of the chapter also looked at this correlation. Out of 51,896 leaders who asked for feedback, the lower 10 percent were rated in the 15th percentile in overall leadership effectiveness. In contrast, those leaders who asked for feedback in the top 10 percent were rated in the 86th percentile in leadership effectiveness. The study ultimately shows that giving and receiving feedback are both imperative skills for effective leaders. People who work for leaders and are open to overall feedback are more engaged and committed.

Four-Step Process in Receiving Feedback

▶ Ask: Make an appointment to meet with your leader on a regular basis. Ask for feedback after each project or event you feel you can improve upon.

▶ Delve: When the person gives you feedback, ask at least three delving questions to find out specifically what they mean.

▶ Next Steps: It is all about how you will implement the advice. Ask what solutions or actions you can take to be better next time. Ask what next steps can you take to improve. Plan "how" you will get there.

▶ Follow-up: Ask when you can follow up with the person to insure that they see your progress and what more you can do to keep improving.

Best Practices in Receiving Feedback

◆ Recognize that any feedback is an opportunity to learn.

◆ Feedback is all around you and you are receiving it all day long, every day.

◆ When you get a project or you are invited to a "by invitation only" meeting, you are receiving feedback.

◆ When you do not get a project or an invitation to the meeting, you are also receiving feedback

◆ Be aware of the intentions of the person, but don't read into them too much.

◆ If you hear feedback from one person you do not respect, hold on to it and evaluate its validity. If you continue to hear the same thing from others, realize that the feedback is valid.

What Not To Do

▶ Avoid getting emotional and displaying emotions such as crying or getting angry or defensive.

▶ Keep your body language open. Do not cross your arms, make negative sounds, or shake your head no.

▶ Do not say anything that you will regret later.

▶ Do not try to make excuses or place blame on other people or events.

▶ Do not talk negatively to colleagues about the person giving you feedback.

▶ Do not disregard the feedback altogether.

Ask Yourself These Crucial Questions

▶ What did you do with any feedback you have received in the last month?

▶ Did you develop a plan of action to improve based on any feedback you have been given recently?

▶ Have you followed up with the person giving you feedback to see if they have noticed any changes?

On the Side

"Normally I listen to the feedback given to me and try and keep an open mind. I don't really ask a lot of questions or talk too much because I don't want to come across as being defensive. What has been frustrating for me in the past is the fact that I feel like I was receptive and went back and implemented what my manager told me to do, but it never seemed like exactly what she wanted.

"After implementing the four-step process that Image Dynamics gave me, everything changed. I realized that asking questions and delving was not being defensive if I did it in an open way with a 'learning attitude.' I started to really delve into what my manager was telling me and really guided her to tell me what specifically she thought I could improve. I had never asked her opinion of 'how' she felt I should change the behavior. This made a world of difference. The feedback really turned into a mentoring session. From there I was able to set a time with her to follow up to evaluate how I was doing. In the past, I waited for review times to receive feedback. Now I feel I'm in a constant growth mode. It's pretty amazing because now my manager has become my mentor and one of my biggest advocates. She even started talking to me about a promotion.

"Making sure I'm in charge of the feedback, as opposed to it only being a one-way deliver, has changed my career."

—IT outsourcing, account manager

Big Mistake 13

Not Adapting to Different Communication Styles

Insanity: doing the same thing over and over again and expecting different results.

—Albert Einstein

"Why must we always communicate? Why can't you just listen to me?"

In today's corporate environment, we are missing an opportunity to better connect when we do not recognize and adapt to different communication styles. We allow ourselves to get frustrated with how other people handle situations, time lines, and conversations. To be most effective, we must realize that people work at different speeds and in different ways.

Let's explore the normal behaviors that we see on a day-to-day basis. We all have natural communication tendencies that can change based on the situation and the environment. Would you agree that some people dominate a conversation and some sit back and listen? Some want all the specific details while others are thinking about who is going to be involved and not wanting to leave people out. Some want to control the project and others want to take a backseat because they do not know enough. Some people are like chameleons, and we are not sure how they like to receive communication because they tend to be very flexible.

There are many assessment tools available that analyze personality styles and provide insight into who we are and how we handle everyday situations and dealings with other people. The key is our own self-awareness. When people are not self-aware, it is very difficult to adapt. After we are self-aware, it is critical that we figure out how other people like to communicate and adapt.

On the Side

"One of the greatest lessons I've learned in my career is the importance of being adaptable when it comes to the communication and personality styles of others. Some people ask, 'Why do *I* have to change my style when *he/she* is clearly the difficult one?!' This is a tough concept to embrace, and requires a fair amount of professional maturity. However, the investment into this skill paves the way to some of the greatest career payoffs I've seen. In addition, I believe it's the responsibility of a strong leader to be able to flex this muscle at any given time.

"Throughout my career, I've seen this form of adaptability pay off in the following ways:

- Gaining buy-in and commitment from others, especially during some of those uphill battles we all face.

- Exerting influence without authority.

- Finding ways to sell your ideas to those who are more senior than you.

- Building trust by creating a comfortable environment in which the other person feels safe to share insights and information.

- Enhancing the performance of your team by delivering development to them in a way that they can more easily process and implement new knowledge and skills.

"The key is to keep it authentic. Being adaptable shouldn't mean losing who you are. It is about enhancing your authentic self so that you can easily and quickly relate to others. Tap into the areas of communication and relationships where you're naturally strong, and make a genuine effort to show continuous improvement in your development areas. After all, if we're not able to play well with others, how far can we possibly go?"

—Erin Bric, manager organization development, VP Action Sports—Vans, Reef & Eagle Creek

The following examples provide an opportunity for you to think about knowing yourself, reading others, and adapting. Keep in mind that you will likely see a little of yourself in all of these people. You may also find yourself relating to some more than others.

Joe: Just get to the bottom line.

Let's talk about Joe. Joe is a get-it-done kind of guy. He tells it like it is, he always wants the bottom line, and he does not like small talk unless he is the one making it. He focuses on accomplishing tasks as quickly as possible. He seems to procrastinate because he has a lot on his plate, and he thrives on the challenge of getting his work done in the nick of time. His desk is messy while he juggles multiple tasks. When asked, he knows where things are, or at least he makes others think he knows. Joe is direct and does not avoid confrontation.

At times it seems as though he does not care about others' feelings because he is so focused on the task rather than the person. Some people would even say that Joe thinks it is all about him. He is really confident and can be intimidating at times. Joe has to be in control. On the other hand, it is fun working with him because of his energy. He loves taking risks. Joe is an asset to the team because he is a visionary who gets things done.

How do you deal with Joe? Here are some best practices:

▶ Stay focused on the bottom line.

▶ Get to the point quickly.

▶ Don't give him all of the details unless he asks, and even then be brief.

▶ Always give him an executive summary with the support information behind it.

▶ Openly admire how well he did a project.

▶ Tell him when you need his help and time rather than asking when he has the time. He never has the time—he's busy.

▶ Listen when he is talking and nod to show you are listening.

Caveat: Joe may not always be task oriented, but when he is working on a project or has a deadline, he definitely seems more focused on the end result. When he has time, he seems to not be as abrupt. This is good to know about Joe. Being aware of where he is in his day and what he has going on helps you figure out how to adapt to him.

Sally: It's all about the people.

Sally works with Joe. Sally is a real people person who is very enthusiastic and energetic. She loves to know what is going on with everyone and everything and likes to feel included. In fact, when she is not included, she seems to get upset. Sally gets to work early to ensure that she is seen and has time to chat with her friends. She is impulsive, taking on any new project she is asked to be a part of, and she hates to say no. Yet finishing the tasks is a different story because she has too much going on all of the time. She loves generating ideas and looks at the people and fun factor of any project. Routine tasks seem tedious and mundane to her.

Sally is the first to say hello in the morning and greets everyone she walks by during the day. She will call or e-mail multiple times because when she has a question, she wants to know the answer right away. Unfortunately, she tends to leave her notes at home. Sally sometimes gets herself in a bind because she likes to gossip. Yet when someone gets angry with her, she gets incredibly upset because she wants everyone to like her. Sally is an asset to the team because of her people skills.

How do you deal with Sally? Here are some best practices:

▶ Take the time to get to know Sally on a personal level. For example, start by asking her about her weekend.

▶ Keep Sally in the loop and include her in meetings.

▶ Ask for her ideas.

▶ Allow her to provide input.

▶ Show interest in her work.

▶ Do not just send her e-mails; invest in face time or time on the phone when possible.

▶ Allow her to work on new projects.

Caveat: Sally may not be as chatty at times. She may either seem like Joe when she is really busy or she may get really quiet and listen to what everyone has to say. Sometimes you are not sure what mode Sally is in and you really have to pay attention. You realize that this may change based on the time of day or what is going on in the office.

Jeff: Steady as it goes.

Jeff is the peacekeeper of the bunch. He does not like to rock the boat at all, although he will if it is necessary. Jeff is concerned about how things affect the team. He likes to make thoughtful decisions and carefully examine all of the ramifications of each decision. Jeff likes to take time to process his thoughts. Everyone in the office knows that they can go to Jeff when they need someone to listen. He always has the patience to hear them and does not need to add his two cents. Jeff is very accommodating most of the time. He does seem to get upset when he has too much on his plate and does not feel that he can finish the job in the specified amount of time. Jeff is methodical and consistent. Jeff is definitely the most interested in how well the team is functioning together and making sure everyone is included when necessary.

How do you deal with Jeff? Here are some best practices:

- When possible, make appointments with Jeff rather than interrupting his work.

- Show respect for his caution in making decisions. He will generally need time to think things over before he makes a decision.

- Make decisions with him collaboratively.

- Have mutually agreed-on deadlines.

- Show a genuine interest in his personal life.

- Understand his need for team input. He does not like to make decisions without being collaborative and weighing all of the options.

- Show sincere appreciation when he does something for you.

- You may have to ask him a couple of times what he thinks about a situation because he will not want to rock the boat.

- Jeff will not "wing-it" or impulsively do something. He likes to do things correctly and takes his time to make sure everything is lined up before he jumps into a project.

Caveat: Jeff always seems methodical. Sometimes, he seems more concerned with the details than anything else. At times he seems better at making decisions than others are at making them. It may get annoying because he wants collaboration. Jeff sometimes seems to care an awful lot about what people think of him while at other times he is less concerned with that and more concerned that you are all "doing the right thing."

Cheryl: It's all about the details.

Cheryl is in the accounting department. She is all about facts, quality, accuracy, and details. Cheryl does not have a lot of time to discuss personal issues with her coworkers. Her privacy is important to her. When she arrives in the morning, she gets to work immediately and does not have the time or the interest to engage in chitchat. Cheryl works hard to make sure that her work is of the highest quality, so when she gets criticized or critiqued, she is not happy. However, she is quick to criticize others when she feels that someone is not doing their job well. When given a report that lacks sufficient detail, Cheryl feels that it is a waste of her time to read it. She consistently asks her coworkers to fill in the details so that her analysis can be more thorough. Cheryl is task oriented and very diplomatic. She really does not enjoy working with people who are outwardly passionate or enthusiastic. She would prefer the facts in a concise manner.

How do you deal with Cheryl? Here are some best practices:

▶ Focus on the facts.

▶ Don't get into your personal issues unless you have a strong personal relationship. Even then she will probably not engage in the conversation too much.

▶ Let her take time to process a decision; do not expect an immediate resolution.

▶ Be specific when being critical or giving suggestions. Realize she will not like what you say because it may offend her drive for perfection. When she feels that something is not perfect, it upsets her.

▶ Be prepared to give the details that back up any overview or summary.

▶ Offer opportunities that let her use her expertise.

Caveat: Cheryl seems to be in the weeds a lot, but then there are other times when she seems like Joe and just wants to get to the bottom line. The best course of action is to always start with the bottom line, but be prepared with the details. Even if she does not want them at that moment, she will want everything documented and available to her.

Analyze This

Joe, Sally, Jeff, and Cheryl were driving to a meeting three hours away. Joe was the driver and Sally was the copilot. Cheryl kept looking over Joe's shoulder, upset that he seemed to be going faster than the speed limit. Joe was annoyed that Cheryl kept making comments. Jeff was a little hungry and pulled out his baggie of labeled carrots and offered some to the group. He had brought enough for everyone. Sally had M&M's and chips. Cheryl had packed a cooler—everything in its place—full of water and sandwiches. Joe was running late so he had no snacks.

As Cheryl ate her sandwich, she looked at Sally and again commented on Joe's speed. Sally just looked at her and smiled; there was no way she was saying anything to Joe. Joe overheard and said to the others, "Stop worrying about my speed! Bottom line, let me do the driving!" And off they went.

Can you tell which parts of their natural communication styles were coming out during the drive? How could you tell?

Best Practices

▶ Figure out how you like to communicate. Self-awareness is the key to all of this.

▶ Know whether someone is a talker or a listener, and adapt accordingly. If they are a talker, let them talk. If they are a listener, ask questions to bring them out.

▶ Be aware if you are talking too much.

▶ Know whether someone is task oriented or people oriented, and try to adapt.

▶ If the other person likes to talk about personal matters, show interest in their lives and then move on to the business at hand.

▶ Realize that most people are not trying to annoy others but are doing what comes naturally to them.

On the Side

"One of my clients is extremely abrupt with others around her. She gets annoyed when people are not on her time schedule. She especially gets upset when her team does not jump into action when she needs something done. One of her peers on the management team is very similar to her and she gets extremely frustrated by him. She cannot believe how her peer speaks to his team. It is very interesting to watch because she has no idea that she is doing the same thing to her team. She has been told that she is too abrupt but insists that other people are incompetent. She really has no self-awarenesss. The sad part is that others do not like to work with her and for her, yet she does not see that and is not open to hearing the feedback."

—Kim Zoller, Image Dynamics

Ask Yourself These Crucial Questions

▶ Do I adapt to other people or do I do what is natural for my communication style?

▶ Do I notice how sometimes I have rapport with others and how sometimes building rapport is difficult?

▶ Can I identify the preferred communication style of everyone I work with and start to adapt to their preferred styles?

Big Mistake 14 \ Not Reacting Professionally

My behavior is my reaction; my reaction is my behavior.

—Unknown

Let's face it: Everyone has times when they get upset and overly emotional. It seems to be easy to pick it out in other people when this happens and less so when it happens to you. Have you ever found yourself reacting to a situation and afterward wish you had handled it differently? You know that you keep repeating a similar reaction and getting the same feeling of annoyance, hurt, frustration, or disdain. You want to change your reaction, but you are just not sure how to do that. You know that this is hurting the impact of your communication and your overall effectiveness with others. We call this "going down the rat hole." Going down the rat hole is when we allow things that negatively trigger us to cause a negative inward or outward reaction.

Stop and think about what is going on in your mind. We react to others because we have a preconceived idea of what they want based on previous experience and assumptions.

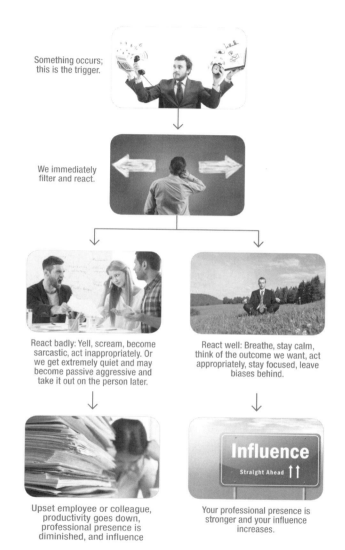

Something occurs; this is the trigger.

We immediately filter and react.

React badly: Yell, scream, become sarcastic, act inappropriately. Or we get extremely quiet and may become passive aggressive and take it out on the person later.

React well: Breathe, stay calm, think of the outcome we want, act appropriately, stay focused, leave biases behind.

Upset employee or colleague, productivity goes down, professional presence is diminished, and influence

Influence
Straight Ahead ↑↑

Your professional presence is stronger and your influence increases.

| I react in the same way to a trigger; it has become my behavior. | What is the trigger? | How do I feel? | What should I do? I want to change the behavior to get a different reaction. | I really want to feel in control—how do I do that?? |

Something happens that triggers a reaction from you and leaves you thinking, "If only I hadn't said…" or "If only I had handled it differently…now I feel so angry, embarrassed, frustrated, and cornered."

Why do we continue to react in the same way, knowing that we will regret our actions later? One cannot stop events that trigger reactions. We can, however, become aware of what is happening and look at our own behavior and reactions. All of us walk around with preconceived ideas or stories in our heads of how things "should" be, how others expect us to be, and what we think we need to show people.

This is all tied into our emotional intelligence. Remember that our emotional intelligence is how we learn to deal with our emotions, as well as others'. Through Daniel Goleman's studies he shows that 85 percent of the differences between a "good leader" and an "excellent leader" is due to emotional intelligence.

Also, it is important to come into all situations from the other person's point of view, situation, or position. This will ultimately help your communication. Listen and learn as opposed to immediately responding or reacting. For example, Harry is talking to Reginald and says, "We are not spending the money on this project. We are going to use it for better things."

Reginald feels immediately upset and starts taking this decision personally. Then he stops, takes a breath, and says "Harry, can you tell me more about your decision? What would qualify as 'better'?"

Slow down, realize it is a trigger, and communicate with the goals to build the relationship, as well as make the best decision.

On the Side

"Bob felt that every time he had to present at an executive meeting, he needed to show how clever he was and how much he had researched the issue. This was the trigger that caused him to go on and on and never get to the point. Unfortunately, the executives in his company started to feel that he did not understand the big picture, when, in reality, Bob thought that all the facts he was giving were showing how much he understood. When Bob recognized this trigger and realized that he did not have to prove how clever he was, he changed his delivery to the executive team. Bob let go of the 'story' in his head. The result was that the executive team at his company now recognizes him as one of the most competent individuals who always 'hits the target.'"

—Harriet Whiting, vice president at Image Dynamics

How Do I Deal With the Triggers?

Best Practices

▶ When you find yourself going down the "rat hole" and not getting results, *stop*.

▶ Write down your triggers—those things that happen around you that cause you to react negatively.

▶ Memorize those triggers and become aware of them immediately.

▶ Be prepared when those triggers happen and know that they will happen.

▶ Set a goal ahead of time to not allow yourself to be triggered. Recognize who sets you off. What can you learn from past experiences with this person or this type of situation?

▶ Stop as soon as you are triggered, take a deep breath, and think about your reaction.

▶ Realize that the "story" in your head may not be reality.

▶ Start noticing how your reactions may trigger others and figure out how to change those reactions.

▶ Be aware of how certain behaviors may trigger your colleagues. For example, getting right to the point without saying hello may trigger a colleague who is a people-oriented person.

▶ If you do not know how to change your behavior, you may want to look into working with an executive coach.

Ask Yourself These Crucial Questions

▶ Have I ever stopped when I find myself reacting negatively and become aware of *how* I am feeling and behaving?

▶ What is triggering my reaction and what can I do to change my reaction?

▶ What do I need to ask to gain more clarity to change my behavior?

Big Mistake 15 〉 Bloopers and Blunders: Saying and Doing the Wrong Thing

Experience is simply the name we give our mistakes.

—Oscar Wilde

This chapter encompasses all of those things we say that could get us into trouble and hurt our relationships and reputations if we do not recover quickly and gracefully.

Have you ever said anything and wished immediately you could take it back? For example, last week I was with a client who I thought was definitely pregnant. Not only did I ask her when she was due, I put my hand on her stomach. I was mortified when she said that she was not pregnant, just had some weight to lose.

Here are a few questions that could get you into trouble if you did not read a situation correctly or said something without thinking first:

▶ "How old are you?"

▶ "What's your religion? Do you go to church?"

▶ "Do you have a girlfriend/boyfriend?"

- ► "Do you have kids?"
- ► "Why don't you drink alcohol?"
- ► "What happened? Why did you get divorced?"
- ► "When are you due?"
- ► "At least your dad was 90 years old when he died. He lived a long life."

If you do say something that you wish you had not, here is a three-step solution to recover:

1. Apologize.
2. Ask for forgiveness for own your inappropriate statement.
3. Learn from your mistakes.

There are other actions that may communicate your brand negatively. Here are a few examples to help keep you out of trouble.

Driving

Be careful that you do not cut people off or use improper body language. Who knows—you could end up in a meeting with the person in the next lane. Obey all traffic rules within the work parking lot or when at a client's place of business.

Waiting in Line

Do not cut in line, and do not say something you will be sorry about as you stand in line. That person you cut in front of or the person who hears you say something rude could be the person interviewing you for a job, your new colleague, or the new VP in your company. This applies to all situations, from the grocery store to checking in at a reception desk at a business.

Traveling

You never know who someone is and where they will turn up. Being on your A-game at all times will only help you. Do not make snide comments about another passenger or the flight attendant on an airplane.

Don't be in such a hurry that you become impolite. Everyone on your plane is going to the same place at the same time. You can't pass someone and get to your destination any faster than they do.

Additionally, if you see that someone may need help, such as stowing a bag in the overhead compartment, ask if you can be of assistance.

Networking Events

You are not there to eat. There is nothing worse than speaking with someone who is talking with their mouth filled with food. Stay positive; no one likes to be around a negative person.

Bathroom

Wash your hands. If you do not, someone else in there with you could come out and tell their friends or colleagues that you didn't.

Restaurants and Stores

Be nice to servers and sales associates. People show their lack of character when they are rude to the person serving them. We may think that rudeness is acceptable when we do not get the service we expect, but it reflects badly on the person with the rude behavior.

Chapter 16

Ask Kim and Kerry: Answers to Sticky Situations

Q. How do I deal with it when I take a day off to unwind and my boss keeps texting me?

A. First, clarify your availability before you take the day off. You are setting the boundary. If you do not do that or do not feel comfortable saying something before you take the time off, you will have to handle it as the texts come in on your vacation day. But, that doesn't mean that you can't still set the boundary. Let your boss know that you got the text and that you will be away from your phone, taking advantage of your day off, and will address and handle everything as soon as you get back into the office. If you keep responding, they will keep asking.

Exception to the rule: If there is something that has to be done immediately, step up and do what you need to do.

Q. What happens when I have communicated a brand that I want to change? Can I?

A. The good news is that you can change your brand, just like a retail product. You will have to do your own brand gap analysis. First, find out what you have communicated and how people see you. Then, map out the brand you are truly trying to represent. Within that, it is imperative to make sure that you know the exact behaviors that represent your desired brand. Sit down with a mentor/role model to get input.

You will then need to start communicating your brand every day. Unfortunately, there can be no setbacks. The minute you revert back to an old way of behaving, people will think, "Oh, she's/he's just back to being how they normally are."

Once you have started living your updated brand, let people know that you are really trying to change and that you realize your old behavior was not effective. The caveat here is if you go back to an old habit too soon, all your work will be in vain.

Q. What do I do if I send an e-mail with typos and don't realize it until later?

A. As soon as you realize the problem, resend the e-mail with an apology and the corrections.

Q. Is it appropriate to forward e-mails to my boss showcasing a "job-well-done" on my behalf?

A. Yes, it is appropriate, but only on occasion. When it is above and beyond or exceptional, you should definitely sing your praises. However, it is not all right to regularly forward accolades about your work. There is a line between exceptional and the expectation of how you do your job.

The other key point to remember is that it is always more beneficial for someone else to say how great you are as opposed to you telling everyone how great you are. You have to know when humility works in your favor.

Q. Should I accept my clients as "friends" on Facebook?

A. Typically, keep your private life private. With that being said, there are exceptions. When you have built a relation-ship that crosses over into a friendship, it may seem dis-ingenuous not to accept the invitation. The one thing to remember is that what you post is always a reflection of you whether your clients are friends or not.

Big Mistake 17 ⟩ Not Communicating Value

A brand is a living entity—and it is enriched or undermined cumulatively over time, the product of a thousand small gestures.

—Michael Eisner

What is value and how does something become valuable? By investing in your brand and the behaviors that support it, you communicate value.

Everything we have put in this book builds your value. Everything and everyone has intrinsic value. You have to communicate your value so that others see you as valuable. Investing in relationships and being aware of best practices for all communication methods and modes builds your value over time.

You build value:

▶ When you help someone else achieve a goal.

▶ When you invest in someone else's growth.

▶ When you spend time learning about another person, their company, their goals, and their needs and wants.

▶ Over time.

▶ When you pay attention to the details.

▶ By remembering the details someone has taken the time to share.

▶ When you go the extra mile.

▶ When you are consistent.

▶ When you do what you say you are going to do.

▶ When you work hard at both your relationship and the actual work.

▶ When you are responsive in a timely manner.

▶ When you listen.

▶ When you are not always selling yourself or your product but are seeking to understand.

▶ When you take the time to pick up the phone or visit someone, not just send an e-mail.

▶ When you send a handwritten note.

▶ When you are not arrogant and a know-it-all.

▶ When you are a learner.

▶ When you think about what you say and how you say it.

▶ When you genuinely care.

We are all unique in the way we communicate. There are strengths and opportunities for growth in everyone's natural style. We have also learned techniques along the way—some good and some not very beneficial—to meet our goals. Good communication is imperative yet it is the one thing most professionals complain about the most.

It is not easy communicating effectively all of the time. As with anything in life, some of our communication will build our brand and some will break it down. The question is: How much are you willing to work on your communication to ensure that you are building strong and positive relationships? Are you willing to recognize that certain things you say and how you say them are ineffective? Will you invest the time to change learned behavior?

Each time you communicate as a professional, you have a choice. When you take the time to think about how you will say something and how you will handle yourself, the chance of meeting your desired outcome increases. We challenge you to do just that. Here's to not leaving any situation and having someone later say, "You said *what*?!"

Chapter 18 〉 Your Action Plan for Continued Success

Any idea is useless unless put into action. We have found that many of the professionals we work with are excellent at the large impactful aspects of their positions but do not take care of the details in their communication. They do not know the "how to's" for putting a book like this into action.

Here is a specific action plan to keep you on track:

1. Write down one to three specific communication goals you have at the moment. For instance, a stronger relationship with a colleague, more effective sales calls, getting a promotion through the feedback you are given, or not saying inappropriate comments at meetings.

2. Write down the key stakeholders who are relevant to your specific goal and what their communication hot buttons are regarding what they expect from you.

3. Go through each chapter with three highlighters. One color signifies what you need to START doing, as it will make a difference in your career. Another

color signifies what you need to CONTINUE doing and may not do consistently. The third color signifies what you need to STOP doing. These are the actions that are stalling or stopping your career growth.

4. With those expectations in mind, take three points from each highlighted color in each chapter and create your behavior action plan.

5. Go through the chapter checklist (see page 116) on a weekly basis. How will you measure your success? Define your performance metrics and follow it monthly. Modify when necessary.

The following is an example of how you can write down your specific action plan and keep track of your goals and accomplishments as you go along.

#1. Goal:

My goal is to learn the communication styles of my team in order to communicate more effectively with them.

#2. Stakeholders and their communication hot buttons:

Michael: Wants things to be direct and to the point.

Srinivas: Likes to make small talk for a few minutes and then get right to the bottom line. Doesn't really like too much detail.

Leigh: Wants to know the details and who is going to be involved. Wants to know any ramification to the team or other key players or stakeholders. Does not like any surprises.

Alex: Wants all of the detail without anything left out. Gets very annoyed when things are dropped on his plate at the last minute and expected to be done immediately.

Sarah: Hard to read. Sometimes she is very chatty and other times she could not care less about what is going on with anyone else. She says she wants all of the details, but then, when you give them to her, she gets distracted and takes out her phone in the middle of the conversation.

#3 & #4 Highlight and write action plan:

Start: Rereading every e-mail I send to make sure that it is sent with each receiver in mind. With Srinivas I will be more chatty; with Michael, I'll be really direct and stop asking him about his weekend, etc.

Continue: Paying attention to the nuances of each person

Stop: Approaching everyone the way I like to be approached. I realize that not everyone wants to get to know me on a personal basis. While this is personally a little hurtful, I am going to take into account that everyone has different styles and different agendas.

#5. Chapter Checklist, Metrics Measuring.

The following list includes examples on how to set up specific behavior metrics in each chapter. Take the time to tailor this to yourself. Each chapter could have many behaviors to support your goal. Print out this list to create your own portable metric checklist.

1. Being on Your A-Game
2. Beginning with the End in Mind
3. Knowing Your Personal Brand
4. Managing Perceptions
5. Connecting and Building Relationships
6. Making Appropriate Small Talk
7. Superb Communication Through Technology Use
8. Managing Your Social Networking

1. Be on My A-Game

✓ Goal: Not to let my personal life affect what is going on at work.

✓ I was so upset with my husband last week, but I put a smile on my face, took a breath, and acted as though everything was fine. It was great, because after about 20 minutes, I actually felt so much better.

2. Begin With the End In Mind

✓ Goal: Plan out my next conversation with my manager.

✓ I sat down the day before my meeting and made a plan outlining his communication preference, all of his hot buttons, the benefits and risks to what I was suggesting and next steps. It worked really well and I am going to do that for every conversation moving forward.

3. Know My Personal Brand

✓ Goal: Realize that how I come across every day reflect my brand.

✓ I have been sitting in my car for a few minutes before walking into work, thinking about my brand and how it is going to be communicated through my actions and especially through my e-mails. It seems to be working really well. I have noticed that my coworkers have been really responsive this week.

4. Manage Perceptions

✓ Goal: To learn about my blind areas so that I can be more aware of the behavior I am doing that could be perceived as negative.

✓ I asked Sam, my cubicle mate, what I did that may not be perceived as positive. He asked me to be more specific. I asked about the professionalism of my conversations. He told me that I was extremely loud and it was sometimes hard for him to concentrate on his own work.

5. Connect and Build Relationships

✓ Goal: To go out of my way to build a relationship with Vicky even though she can be so abrupt at times.

✓ I was able to have a one-on-one conversation with Vicky at the meeting and she is actually terrific. We have a lot in common and I realized that she is abrupt because she has a huge amount of responsibility and that is how she communicates her stress. I will not take it personally anymore.

6. Make Appropriate Small Talk

✓ Goal: To go to that networking event and meet at least one new person.

✓ I went to the Wine & Wisdom Association event and I told my colleague I would see her at the end of the evening. That was really hard. I then used my planned conversation tactics and had three good conversations with people I will follow up with this week. I concentrated on "being interested, not interesting." This made it so much easier for me because I didn't have to come up with a lot to say, but I was able to build on what they were saying.

7. Superb Communication Through Technology Use

✓ Goal: Not send any emotional e-mails.

✓ I put three emails into my draft folder this week and waited an hour to reread them before sending. I was so glad I did that because they would have been seen as extremely rude and emotional if I had sent them.

8. Manage My Social Network

✓ Goal: To take the time to think about what I can post on LinkedIn that would make an impact on my sales.

✓ I wrote a value-added Top Ten Tips for how to choose a printing company this week. When I posted it, the response was amazing. I am going to take the time even more now to think about what I am posting.

9. Awareness of Communication Stallers and Stoppers

✓ Goal: Not to say, "I can't do it" the minute someone wants to give me another piece of work.

✓ I thanked Jacques for giving me the opportunity and asked him for more information about the data needed. When I found out the details, I realized I was able to do it and I was glad that I had not immediately said no, which was my first instinct.

10. Not Make Assumptions

✓ Goal: To not think that people are doing things to hurt me. Stop the ANTs.

✓ I wanted to tell Bill what I thought about him when he forwarded my e-mail to his boss. But, I didn't. Instead, I went to talk to him directly and calmly to find out his thoughts and why his boss needed to be included. When he explained to me his boss's role, I understood why he had sent it and realized that it had nothing to do with me, but with the outcome of the project. I felt so much better.

11. Focus on the Details

✓ Goal: To presenting my weekly PowerPoint more professionally.

✓ I took the time to go through my PowerPoint and make sure all the fonts were the same and there were no typos. I also made sure that the slides looked clean and communicated my message well. I took the time to think about what I was wearing for the Wednesday meeting. It felt great when the VP came up to me after the meeting to tell me how professional I was and how he was so impressed with me.

12. Give and Receive Precise Feedback

✓ Goal: To not be defensive when I get feedback on my monthly report.

✓ I sat down with Belinda and was totally open to her feedback on Friday. When she said that she saw some mistakes, I asked for very specific information and asked for her thoughts on how she would do it. She actually gave me a great idea that will take me less time.

13. Adapt to Different Communication Styles

✓ Goal: To make sure I get an e-mail response when I ask for information.

✓ I sat down and analyzed what would make Sue respond to me faster. When I realized that Sue reads e-mails with bullet points that are concise and my e-mails were too long, I changed my format. She immediately sent me back what I needed.

14. React Professionally

✓ Goal: To not get triggered when people don't like my ideas.

✓ I did not get visibly upset when Laura did not appreciate all the work I had put into her project and felt that more needed to be done. I calmly asked her for more information and she thanked me for not taking it personally and being focused on the goal. I could tell she was worried that I would take it personally from our previous encounters. That was eye opening for me.

15. Do and Say the Right Thing

✓ Goal: To have more of a verbal filter with my colleagues.

✓ I really wanted to ask Sally if she was pregnant. She looked pregnant and I know she has been trying. But, I didn't, and I thought to myself, "I'll find out if she is when she wants to tell people."

16. Communicate Value

✓ Goal: To make sure that the management team sees value in what I bring to the table and how I always do what I say I will do.

✓ I made sure that I sent follow-up notes to everyone this week even when I didn't know status. This let them know I had not forgotten. It was nice when they thanked me in the Friday meeting.

17. My Action Plan for Continued Success

✓ Goal: Take the time to sharpen and improve my communication skills. I am always so busy that I do not take time to plan how I am communicating my brand, as well as how I communicate to reach my intended outcome.

✓ I scheduled 30 minutes on Friday to go through my checklist to see if I had met my goals from last week and to see if I needed to revise them for the following week.

Bibliography

Adams, Susan. "Networking Is Still the Best Way to Find A Job, Survey Says." June 7, 2011, Forbes.com: *www.forbes.com/sites/susanadams/2011/06/07/networking-is-still-the-best-way-to-find-a-job-survey-says/*.

Argyris, Chris. *Overcoming Organizational Defenses: Facilitating Organizational Leadership.* Boston: Allyn and Bacon, 1990.

Bar, Moshe, Maital Neta, and Heather Linz. "Very first impressions." *Emotion* vol. 6, 2 (2006): 269–278.

Carducci, Bernardo J. *The Pocket Guide to Making Successful Small Talk: How to Talk to Anyone, Anytime, Anywhere About Anything.* Pocket Guide Publishing, 1999.

Derks, D., and A. Bakker. "The Impact of E-mail Communication on Organizational Life." *Cyberpsychology: Journal of Psychosocial Research on Cyberspace,* 4 vol. 1 (2010).

Folkman, Joseph. "The Best Gift Leaders Can Give: Honest Feedback." December 19, 2013, Forbes.com: *www.forbes.com/sites/joefolkman/2013/12/19/the-best-gift-leaders-can-give-honest-feedback/*.

Horowitz, Jason. "Valerie Jarrett's latest role: Shoring up Obama's support base." October 25, 2011. Washingtonpost.com: *www.washingtonpost.com/politics/whitehouse/valerie-jarretts-latest-role-shoring-up-obamas-support-base/2011/10/17/gIQARiI0GM_story.html*.

Luft, Joseph, and Harry Ingham. "The Johari window, a graphic model of interpersonal awareness." In *Proceedings of the Western Training Laboratory in Group Development*. Los Angeles: UCLA, 1955.

Mehrabian, Albert, and Morton Wiener. "Decoding of inconsistent communications." *Journal of Personality and Social Psychology* 6 (1967): 109–114.

Mehrabian, Albert, and Susan R. Ferris. "Inference of attitudes from nonverbal communication in two channels." *Journal of Consulting Psychology* 31 (1967): 248–252.

Senge, Peter M. et al. *The Fifth Discipline Fieldbook: Strategies and Tools for Building a Learning Organization.* New York: Currency, Doubleday, 1994.

Stewart, Greg L.; Susan L. Dustin, Murray R. Barrick, Todd C. Darnold. "Exploring the handshake in employment interviews." *Journal of Applied Psychology* 93 (2008): 1139–1146.

Index

About the Authors

KIM ZOLLER and KERRY PRESTON are recognized experts in leadership development, sales, training, customer service, presentation and communication skills." . They lead Image Dynamics, an innovative professional development organization that collaborates with companies to develop their people and processes. They provide results-oriented training solutions, customized training programs, advanced executive coaching, customer surveys, and long-term strategic development.

Both Kim and Kerry are dynamic international speakers who assist individuals and companies with the necessary tools to be successful in today's competitive market. Over the last two decades, they have trained more than 100,000 individuals.